Mortgages on Paradise

WALTER D. WAGONER

D1651924

ABINGDON
Nashville

MORTGAGES ON PARADISE

Library of Congress Cataloging in Publication Data

WAGONER, WALTER D
  Mortgages on paradise.
  1. Sermons, American. 2. United Church of Christ—Sermons. I. Title.
  BX9886.Z6W335   252'.05834   80-20138

ISBN 0-687-27220-3 (pbk.)

MANUFACTURED BY THE PARTHENON PRESS AT
NASHVILLE, TENNESSEE, UNITED STATES OF AMERICA

To the patient friends and parishioners at the Asylum Hill Congregational Church in Hartford and the Round Hill Community Church in Greenwich—who put me in mind of Mark Twain's words: "I have never heard a sermon from which I didn't derive some good—but I have had some near misses!"

Contents

Preface: Preaching in Context   9

1. Is Happiness a Hoax?   15
2. The Wheel of Change   20
3. Labeled and Done For   25
4. At Home in the Universe   30
5. The Mind Beside Itself   36
6. On Pleading Guilty   42
7. A Lively Time   48
8. Aging and the Generations   54
9. God and Pandemonium   59
10. When the World Gets Out of Hand   64
11. The Packaged Person   70
12. On Coping with Grief   75
13. Mortgages on Paradise   80
14. A Religious World Record   85
15. How Willing Is God?   91
16. On Living with Insoluble Problems   96
17. On Cooling It   102
18. Christmas and the Real World   108
19. On Going Aside   114
20. Living with Fear   120

Preface:
Preaching in Context

Preaching in any situation, be it parish, cathedral, college chapel, or seminary, is at its most effective, I submit, when the preacher knows the congregation and is, therefore, in close touch with the daily lives and real problems of the listeners. Too much preaching, not being related to the human situation, is like the lady in the bank who asked in a loud voice, "Did anyone just lose a large roll of bills?" "Yes," came a shout from an anxious man. "Well, I just found the rubber band!" Far too many sermons, without context, are just as much an empty letdown.

Each of us, of course, has listened to splendid sermons by visiting preachers and imported pulpiteers. Yet, in most such cases, their words have a slight theatrical shimmer, as if the Reverend Big had rushed into the chancel after having been given the five-minute warning in an offstage dressing room.

The preaching that I much prefer is from friend to friend, pilgrim to pilgrim. This is true whether the style be biblical or topical, formal or informal. No preaching, surely, is compelling and persuasive unless it has resulted from three factors: (1) a personal and scholarly wrestling with the Bible, (2) an understandable, compelling vocabulary and speaking style, and (3) an accurate sensitivity to the world in which the laity lives.

Contextual preaching, thus, is not simply an idea or a manifesto or even a biblical text which speaks only to the preacher and then is unilaterally hurled at the expectant congregation. How many times I have made that mistake, saying to myself, "Here's a marvelous sermon idea," and then preached it without investigating its relevance to the congregation. The pulpit is the last place in the world where such narcissism is to flourish—any homiletical self-infatuation with one's own ideas *in vacuuo*.

Thus, the sermons in this volume spring from actual parish settings. Each of them has been triggered by a definite issue or problem, hope or anxiety, which I knew to be present in at least some of the congregation and which I estimated to be of general enough applicability to justify its public presentation. Parishioners with unique or eccentric problems are not a reliable source for such preaching.

These sermons have been preached in one or the other of two fine churches: the Asylum Hill Congregational Church, Hartford, Connecticut, and, on another hill, the Round Hill Community Church in Greenwich, Connecticut. In both parishes the members do not take lightly to "preachy" bromides or sentimental religiosity.

A final word: these sermons reflect, in the usual fashion of most on-the-run parish ministers, illustrations and allusions both original and plagiarized (quotes, clippings, and anecdotes taken from magazines and books as well as personal experiences). What I have tried to add is a consistency of style (saying it *my* way) and adequate knowledge of the situation. There is one clear warning about this type of "felt-need" preaching; namely, the preacher must constantly review the subject matter of the sermons in order to make sure (as one knows the Bible, the creeds, and the lectionary) that major topics which may not always be consciously felt are not forgotten.

I am indebted to the critical cooperation of my friend, Edmund Linn, of the faculty of the Andover-Newton Theological School.

Walter D. Wagoner
Greenwich, Connecticut 1980

Mortgages on Paradise

1. Is Happiness a Hoax?

The Parish Setting

This sermon easily could backfire. There is so much unhappiness in the world that the church's insistence on critically examining current notions of happiness runs in the face of public demand. Also, in centuries past the church often expounded a dour rather than a realistic view of how much happiness is possible to our human condition. One wit, tired of the old overearnest Calvinism, said, "John Calvin appears to his disciples to have been as much like the God of the Old Testament as his health would permit." I recall, similarly, an art historian commenting that "most portraits of the medieval saints look as if they were suffering from acute indigestion."

Such an imbalanced tradition is not consonant with the joy and fulfillment of life in Christ. Yet there lingers in the parish a residual guilt about being both a Christian and *too* a happy person.

If in the past the church has been too grim, today, at the other extreme, the media everywhere touts instant happiness. There are hundreds of therapy groups which promise that happiness can be swallowed without being chewed. Worse, there are churches that glibly equate Jesus to automatic earthly contentment—the most unblushing exponents of this being on TV.

The pews are filled with people desperately seeking happiness, too often starved for it. The problem of this Christian sermon, therefore, is how to distinguish between valid, Christian forms of happiness as over against the hoaxes served to the gullible.

The Sermon   *Text: Isaiah 60*

Hugh McNatt of San Antonio, Texas, recently sued his hometown church for a refund of his eight-hundred-dollar yearly pledge. McNatt charged that he had donated the money in response to the pastor's promise that in return would flow "blessings, benefits, and rewards from God." McNatt had had no such luck!

Actually, McNatt has a point. Too many Christian churches frown on happiness, as if someone were having more fun than sin permitted. There is nothing wrong with happiness, and I wish to God each and all of us had a larger portion of it.

But what is the proper relation of the church and our faith to the pursuit of and enjoyment of happiness?

The word *happiness* is found only once in the Old Testament, where the writer of the book of Lamentations moans that he has "forgotten what happiness is" (3:17*b*). And the word *happiness* is not found anywhere in the New Testament, although that testimony bursts with the allied feelings of joy and fulfillment and exhilaration.

What I find in the biblical testimony and in the tradition of our faith with regard to happiness is this:

First, God wants us to be happy, in the sense that pain and malice and moroseness are clearly out of keeping with the nature of Christ. Christians are to be realistic about the limits of being mortal, about sin, and about suffering, but it is surely non-Christian for us to be essentially gloomy and sick of life. Perhaps the closest parallel to happiness in the mouth of Jesus would be the word *blessed,* as in "blessed are the pure in heart."

Christianity is not an unhappy religion. Brendan Behan, the Irish writer, took fair aim at such unhappy corruptions of Christ when he wrote that most of the crucifixes in his hometown reminded him of sickly young Italian men suffering from overexposure to the sun.

Second, those who stay close to Jesus Christ acquire, I trust, a great deal of wisdom about phony forms of happiness. Happiness can be a lollipop word, one which glibly equates happiness with only sensate materialism or trivial pleasure—ego massage.

Six centuries before Christ, the prophet Isaiah spoke to a scattered and broken people. He summoned them with a vision of a restored people seeking righteousness, with God as their light. He was not promising a life of cookie and crackerjack happiness. When Jesus summoned people, he gave them a magnificent, a terrifying, overwhelming vision of seeking justice, and loving, and a world of peace where laughter and suffering, death and reconciliation were going to be mixed in unforeseeable proportions. These Christians were animated by loyalties and visions that "took them over"; come what may, there was no whimpering over monthly quotas of happiness.

There is a relevant story about a man who died and opened his eyes in the next world. As he looked around, his first thought was, "It could have been worse." He saw beauty, luxury beyond his dreams. An obliging attendant provided instant service for every whim. After a while, however, the man grew restless and impatient. He longed for the variety of simple refusal. One day he confronted his attendant with a demand, "I want something that I can't have without earning it." The attendant replied that he was sorry but that that particular wish could not be granted. Whereupon the man shouted out, "In that case, I will stay here no longer. I would much prefer to go to hell." Whereupon came the answer, "And where do you think you are, sir?"

Finally, our Christian faith, although it should bring us a deep and lasting inward happiness, and though God surely desires that each of us have enough of the things of this world to make for health and well-being, is a faith in which the direct pursuit of happiness is not the main goal. True happiness, such as we may get in this life, is the indirect consequence of a life of usefulness. This is a life that embraces sorrow and joy, pain and death, love and hostility, and does not fret about the Geiger count on the happiness meter. Christ obviously brought enormous happiness to those around him who believed in him. But it was a happiness in the midst of incompleteness and pain and all the varieties of the human condition.

An American college teacher, returning from a sabbatical in a distant country, laughingly recalled a crate that he saw on a railroad platform. It had this large label on it: "This case should be carried bottom upward—the top is labeled bottom to avoid confusion." From whichever angle it is viewed, happiness—that inner joy in being alive in God's world—is not a hand-delivered piece of luggage that one can order and pay for. For the Christian, it is a by-product of a useful, serving, committed life.

> If happiness hae not her seat
> An' centre in the breast,
> We may be wise, or rich, or great,
> But never can be blest.
>   Robert Burns, *Epistle to Davie*

2. The Wheel of Change

The Parish Setting

A sermon on change immediately will arouse the attention of a congregation, so long as it is not delivered in the languid platitudes of a Commencement address. Incidentally, I find that, no matter what the topic, if the sermon doesn't reach out and catch the attention of the listeners within the first two or three sentences, the congregation is gone for the duration—their minds wandering to golf or gardening or oven settings for quiche Lorraine.

It is a mistake to think that only older parishioners are interested in change. This sermon, for example, was stimulated by a conversation with an eighteen-year-old who was astounded at the startling change between his way of life and that of his twelve-year-old brother. Everyone talks about "how much life is changing."

How does one balance stability and flux? How much change can the human psyche absorb without flying apart? How fast should churches change? The process-theologians assert that God is changing. In what sense is Jesus Christ always the same, yesterday, today, and tomorrow? Is anything fixed?

The Sermon   *Text: II Corinthians 4:7-18*

In October 1917, there exploded the most powerful political bomb of the twentieth century: the Revolution in Russia, which deposed the monarchy, established the dictatorship of the proletariat, and ushered in the ruthless figures of Lenin and Stalin. From 1917 to 1937 more than twenty million Russians were killed in domestic purges. Not since the French Revolution had the world seen such a cataclysmic political eruption.

That revolution is worth careful pondering by Christians, as we live in times of tumultuous change. The Russian Orthodox Church, for example, offered in 1917 no alternative to the violence and injustice on its doorsteps. It was more concerned with liturgy and vestments than with justice. The Czar, the national head of the Orthodox Church, was equally insensitive. During the three months preceding the coup d'etat, his chief minister pleaded with him to realize what was making up in Petrograd: the cold, the anger, the plotting, the misery. The Czar replied, "Don't bother me, I want to continue my domino game."

Today Petrograd is called Leningrad.

The members of this church living in a typical American city do not want violent change, much less revolution. But on what scale do we want change in our lives? We may try to beg off grappling with change, but change is too rampant today to permit escape. As Adam said to Eve, as they were being banished from the garden, "This is a time of transition."

We become anxious about change when it comes too fast to handle and when we feel that our basic values and beliefs and way of life are being threatened. Christians, as with others, are not exempt from such anxiety. Yet our faith ought to enable us to handle change with more than usual insight.

One of the most startling examples of change can be seen in certain modern cities in Australia, not far from the lands set aside for the aborigines whose culture has changed very little in thirty-thousand years. When an aborigine comes to the anonymity of the concrete city he is de-tribalized and bewildered. All of us, I am certain, Christian or not, often feel as confused and terrified by change. What reasonably should be expected of Christians in times of shifting values and mystifying change?

First, the followers of Jesus Christ, who brought about more changes than anyone else in human history, are to welcome the right changes and to oppose the wrong. This assertion is rooted in these words: "When anyone is joined to Christ he is a new being; the old is gone, the new has come (II Cor. 5:17 TEV). Or, as voiced by Isaiah: "Cease to dwell on days gone by / and to brood over past history. / Here and now I will do a new thing" (Isa. 43:19 NEB). We Christians are a changed people. We are not to be afraid to advocate change which is in accord with our conscientious Christian judgment. Never, as Christians in a world of challenge and change are we, like the Czar, to sit about merely playing dominoes.

W. C. Fields, the movie comedian, was defeated all his life by dogs and by children—hating both with a thorough malevolence. Once he had to make a movie with a famous baby star, Baby LeRoy. As the infant was carried onto the set, Fields looked at the little scene-stealer with deep distrust and said, "Your line is goo-goo. Don't muff it." As Christians we have something far better to do than to sit in the midst of life's change muttering, "Goo-goo." The most startling thing about Rip Van Winkle was not that he slept for twenty years, but that he slept through the American Revolution, the biggest change in American history.

The second attitude toward change which characterizes Christians is that we be fully engaged in the church because it is anchored in the changeless and yet always calling us to change. It is in the church that we find which values are anchored in God, what is transient, and what is lasting.

Without this community of faith we truly would be shaken by change, because we would not have a steady place whereon to stand. The church is an extraordinary mixture of change and stability. A few years ago I was a guest speaker at the annual meeting of a Boston church. We were welcoming a new, young minister. At the same table with me was an elderly man, in his nineties, who had been Franklin D. Roosevelt's roommate at Harvard. He rose to his feet and said (in a most unRooseveltian manner), "I want to tell our green young minister that nothing in this church ever changes—or should!" That man couldn't have been more wrong, more transfixed by the past.

It is here, in this Christian community, that we are in touch with the changeless, the transcendent, the abiding. When we are not certain which changes are good or bad, or when we feel that change rushes at us too fast, it is here in this church that we always can stop for a moment to pray, "O thou who changest not, abide with me."

3. Labeled and Done For

The Parish Setting

It is sad to realize the degree to which all of us are imprisoned by the labels that others pin on us. Indeed, the whole trend of our academic culture (sociology and psychology in particular) is to categorize us into everything from "inner-directed" to "upper-middle-class." Students are increasingly graded and sorted. I remember a college teacher commenting, "She is eighty-twoish." One result of all this is that therapists spend hours reassuring their anxious clients that they are more than the sum total of the adjectives and pejorative labels stuck on them like decals.

Why do we indulge ourselves in so much labeling? Some labeling reflects the testing and measurement syndrome. Often, more perversely, labeling is done by those who wish to be superior—to "dispose of another." Or, categorizing is done because the facile use of adjectives is an escape from thinking fairly about the whole person: "She is rich and white." "He is a Philistine."

In the parish I constantly run across persons who are upset because they have been labeled a "loser" or "a hopeless conformist" or a "radical." Because hundreds of people are unfairly labeled there are many doors they cannot open in life. It is heartbreaking to watch such people, prejudicially tagged, pound futilely for the rest of their lives on rooms that have been sealed off to them.

This sermon, then, is one attempt to respond to these cries of hurt. It claims that each of us is basically a whole human being, that labels are secondary and partial and often wrong, and that we have the authority of Jesus to shun debasing labeling.

The Sermon   *Text: Mark 5:1-20*

I am told that if I desire to be a great painter there are two things that I must do. First, I must be able to paint well, to have mastered the techniques. Second, I must know where to sit. That is, what angle of vision, which perspective will produce an expressive and excellent composition.

I know, as you do, people of marked ability who always seem to be sitting in the wrong position. They sulk in the shadows, or with light over the wrong shoulder. There was once a school of portrait photography which was like that. The camera was placed in such a position that everyone appeared to have nostrils like woodchuck holes and large pores that only a dermatologist could love.

For exmple, here sits a woman with the very best in ability and education, but all that she can see are mistakes and foibles. We all have met people like that in our travels. No matter how stunning the view—be it Niagara Falls or Bruges—there is always one person in the crowd whose only remark is, "Isn't the coffee terrible?"

The main characteristic of Jesus in this regard is that he always located himself, always "sat," precisely at that point where he clearly and truly saw others for what they were. To Jesus, even Judas was more than a traitor; the thieves on the crosses were human. It is not easy to see people first as humans instead of as adjectives and categories. A label swallows the person when I say, "John Smith is a radical" or, "June Stevenson is uptight." We begin to pigeonhole people, to indulge in "hardening of the categories."

Churches are not exempt from the tyranny of adjectives. There are always moments when sharp debate or deep differences will result in polarization and name-calling. Adjectives take over; humans are lost sight of, and the result is serious damage to the fellowship. Take, for example, this article from the *Chicago Sun-Times,* January 20, 1968:

"There's Nobody Here But Us Christians"

A long simmering dispute over a church timetable broke out Friday when two priests were attacked by a crowd of worshipers in the rectory of St. Nicholas Church. Father

> Glynn was cut and bruised: Father Bilinsky was pinned to the
> rectory floor by irate parishioners. Four persons, including a
> physician, were arrested as some 25 policemen quelled the
> disturbance. Two hundred persons threw snowballs at the
> rectory door, amidst shouts of police brutality. A policeman
> charged that the doctor had bitten him.

I am glad to say that I have never been connected with a church where adjectives got that far out of hand!

From where Jesus sat he was always talking to this *person* or that, not only to a Pharisee or a prostitute or a sinner. How, then, can we tell if we are regarding other persons in a balanced, fair, and Christian manner?

Like Jesus, we should always keep in mind the whole person and only give limited and critical credence to the adjectives. If Jesus had looked upon Zacchaeus only as a tax-gatherer, we would not have a gospel but a sociological survey. In which case Jesus would have answered the dinner table question, "What went on today?" by replying, "Oh, I ran into the usual bunch of characters: a blind man, an adulteress, two stuffy priests, and a handful of bothersome children."

People, sad to say, get used to being treated as adjectives. A child can be labeled as a "failure" early in life and honestly think himself or herself a failure for years to come. "Labeled and Done For." "Who's Johnny?" "Johnny is a failure." End of Johnny.

Jesus often met people with this cringing labeled view of themselves. In Luke's Gospel, when Simon Peter saw the miracle that Jesus performed in catching so many fish, he fell down at Jesus' knees saying, "Depart from me, for I am a *sinful* man, O Lord" (Luke

5:8, italics mine). Peter assumed that because of the adjective *sinful* that Jesus would have nothing to do with him. Instead, Jesus said, "Do not be afraid; henceforth you will be a fisher of men" (Luke 5:10). On another occasion, the scripture reading for today, Jesus met a man possessed by demons. When he saw Jesus he fell before him and cried with a loud voice, "What have you to do with me, Jesus, Son of the Most High God? I adjure you . . . do not torment me" (Mark 5:7). The whole assumption of this poor, agonized man, suffering from a form of mental illness, was that since others knew he was mad and had tormented him because of it, Jesus, the Son of God, surely would torment him most of all. But Jesus, who in his own temptation crisis had overcome the evil spirits, was able to seek out the essential human dignity within the demoniac and not hold him at arm's length.

Jesus, in his assault on everything that cheapens humanity—an assault that took him to the cross—insisted that each one of us is more than the sum total of our labels. In the second chapter of John it is written of Jesus: "He knew men so well, all of them, that he needed no evidence from others about a man, for he himself could tell what was in a man" (verse 25 NEB). None of us can claim to match the insight of Jesus, but because Jesus Christ had that insight none of us is condemned to be only what others say we are, or what we say we are. And because God in Christ loves us, we are the better able to understand who we really are.

4. At Home in the Universe

The Parish Setting

Easter has its glorious "givenness." Christian preachers must address, without circumlocution, the central affirmation of the faith.

Of all the Christian festivals, it is Easter which sends me back to the Bible and to the commentaries more than any other. That is so because, although the resurrection is the very foundation of my personal faith in Jesus as the Christ, Easter is more misunderstood by Christians than is Christmas.

Is the focus of Easter preaching to be a "new life and re-birth" in a purely worldly sense of renewal? Or is it to be a vague notion of Greek immortality? What is the Christian understanding of life everlasting? Is Easter primarily a homage to the dead, replete with lilies? Is it a musical hallelujah chorus, with all the organ stops out? Should the main emphasis be on Easter as the conclusive validation of Christ as God's true messenger and incarnation?

Early in my ministry my Easter sermons were propositional arguments: three points about empty tombs and *why* we should believe in life everlasting.

I have given up that approach (although it is appropriate for forums and discussion). Now I celebrate and proclaim Easter. I don't attempt to prove it. Let the liturgy, the music, carry the day. The sermon is then a well-prepared personal testimony to the living Christ and to life everlasting.

The Sermon   *Text: Luke 24:13-25*

Our apprehension of the power and truth of Easter is related directly to our ability to hear and to appreciate crucial religious signals originating outside of our minds, coming from God. The message of Easter is not a piece of our own philosophy. But we must be able to receive that message. I illustrate.

A few years ago the St. Louis Symphony went to the zoo to give a concert for the animals. It was a scientific experiment to see how animals, birds, and reptiles respond to music. The orchestra played everything from Mozart to the Beatles, while the scientists noted the reactions. Some animals disliked music of all kinds. Most of them were turned off by music in a minor key. Crocodiles, scorpions, and spiders were the only ones that tolerated all kinds of music; while seals liked everything except jazz. In general it was found that animals, reptiles, and insects have a dim receptivity to music. Only humans have a sense gate which opens to a wide musical range.

So, too, with Christianity. Faith—particularly our receptivity to Easter—needs an open sense gate. There are, if you will, crucial religious chords and melodies that require a special opening into our minds and hearts.

A prevailing difficulty, obviously, for Christian faith today is that for many modern people their sense gates open up only to messages from the physical, measurable, scientific data of the universe. Indeed, the disciples on the road to Emmaus were so earthbound—their sense gates so closed to God—that even they for several hours did not recognize Jesus. Their eyes were kept from recognizing him (Luke 24:16).

The resurrection assertions at the very core of our faith *assume*—indeed, are totally grounded on the conviction that there is more to reality than physical phenomena. If we pay attention only to biological-chemical-physical data, Easter will seem to be a confusing compound of wishful thinking and Christian nostalgia. For example, I read recently of a fascinating debate between astrophysicists concerning whether the universe gives any evidence of a creator God. The scientists were divided on the issue. As a believer in God, I naturally was sympathetic with the mathematician who said that to deny creation of the universe to God was like explaining the Oxford English Dictionary by an explosion in a print shop, with all the type falling into place purely by chance. The point is that, confronting the same physical universe, some scientists seem to have a sense gate that admits God—and others do not.

Those who live solely within scientific dimensions of life, without any open door to the supernatural, remind me of that colorful socialite and gourmet society reporter, Lucius Beebe. Beebe reveled in the good life, lavish meals, and name-dropping. His particular fetish was to insist that table wines be served precisely at room temperature. The high life finally got to Beebe, however, and his stomach rebelled. One of his lady friends was told that Beebe was soon to go into the hospital for abdominal surgery. "Well," she replied, "I do hope the doctors have the good grace to open Lucius at precisely room temperature."

That's quite to the point. I know scores of people who live only "at room temperature," live only in this world, who are totally unaware of other temperatures, spiritual dimensions. Why do we live so often only at room temperature—at world temperature, as if this observable world were the only reality?

The message on this very special day is one transmitted to us directly from God, through the historical events of Holy Week. God has said to us in the life and death and resurrection of Jesus Christ that this universe is an everlasting home. God has validated Jesus as God's true messenger. And what we have heard from Jesus, what we have seen in his resurrection, makes the universe a home, a loving and everlasting home, not an alien land.

There is not a pessimistic note in the New Testament after the resurrection.

Easter is, above all else, *the* most important word from God.

The Easter proclamation is twofold: *first,* Jesus is the Messiah, the decisive person in history, the key to understanding the nature and destiny of humanity; *second,* as God's true messenger, Jesus taught and believed in life everlasting. He did so, not out of wishful thinking, but because life everlasting is consonant with the nature of God's eternal love. God did not make us simply and only for death.

It was Wordsworth, I believe, who admonished us to remember that it would be blasphemy to say that we have more of love in our nature than has God. Jesus said, "If you then, being evil, know how to give good gifts to your children, how much more shall your Father who is in heaven" (Matt. 7:11 NAS); "in my Father's house are many mansions" (John 14:2 KJV).

Let me say, at this point, that there are several forms of so-called immortality which, while partially true, are not the same as life everlasting: (1) I am "somewhat" immortal because my genes are passed on to the next generation—true—but that is biological inheritance, not life everlasting; (2) I am "somewhat" immortal because for a time after my death I will be remembered and my influence felt within a small circle—true—but that is not life everlasting.

Life everlasting is the personal continuation of you and me in some intelligent, fulfilling, and glorious way, beyond our present imagining.

How can we possibly imagine the nature of life everlasting? Suppose that you had only the ability to taste, that you could not *see* a sunset, not *hear* the birds, not *speak* to a friend . . . and then suddenly you were given all those faculties. Some such leap of life and apprehension must be involved, beyond our conceiving: "Eye hath not seen, nor ear heard, neither have entered into the heart of man, the things which God hath prepared for them that love him" (I Cor. 2:9 KJV).

My words limp. I quote, instead, the pen of Thomas Wolfe in *You Can't Go Home Again:*

> Something has spoken in the night, and told me I shall die, ... Saying:
> "To lose the earth you know, for greater knowing; to lose the life you have, for greater life; to leave the friends you loved, for greater loving; to find a land more kind than home, more large than earth—
> "—Whereon the pillars of this earth are founded, toward which the conscience of the world is tending—a wind is rising, and the rivers flow."

Today we celebrate Christ as the true Son of God. We do this surrounded by the Christian church in every land and surrounded by the glorious company of heaven who respond to our song, "He is risen!" with their eternal chorus, "Hallelujah, He is risen indeed!"

5. The Mind Beside Itself

The Parish Setting

The subject matter of this sermon resulted from a poll of a church-governing board, asking which subjects they wanted sermons to address.

Anger, hate, and hostility were high on almost every list. There are obvious reasons for this priority: (1) each of us has to deal (or refuse to deal) with these emotions, (2) the church is filled with talk about love and kindness as virtues to such a degree that members are guilty or intimidated by the fact that they have, as all humans, contrary emotions. So many people unfortunately believe that if one is a Christian or a good person, one is not supposed to have hateful and destructive feelings.

Sermons on powerful emotions, such as anger and hate, will be only partial therapy. With luck, the sermon and related discussion groups and prayer will open up the subject, help reduce defensive and suppressive mechanisms, as well as having the virtue of the minister saying publicly, "I get angry, you get angry, let's face it."

The Sermon   *Text: Matthew 5:21-26*

In the midst of so many crises, both foreign and domestic, the national "psychic temperature" of America rises. This is paralleled in the frayed and raw condition of personal anger and anxiety. There is a rock music song with these words:

> The whole world is festering with unhappy souls
> The French hate the Germans
> The Germans hate the Poles
> Italians hate Yugoslavs
> South Africans hate the Dutch
> And I don't like anybody very much.

I, therefore, preach today on personal anger—from what I hope is a valid Christian perspective. Doing the right thing with our personal angers relates only partially to the strategies needed for political animosities. But when we see how difficult it is to handle ourselves, we can understand how intractable are nations.

As Christians, knowing that by the example of Christ we are intended to live by love and forgiveness, we are often embarrassed by our anger and feel guilty. But we do feel anger. Any attempt to deny that, or constantly to suppress it, is sheer obtuseness. What we have to do as Christians is to figure out how to handle personal anger in such a way that reconciliation is possible.

In *Huckleberry Finn* Huck is washed up on the Arkansas shore of the Mississippi and finds himself in the midst of a shoot-out between families. Told that it was a feud, Huck asks the farmer, Buck, "What's a feud?"

"Well," says Buck, "a feud is this way: A man has a quarrel with another man, and kills him; then that other man's brother kills *him*; then the other brothers, on both sides, goes for one another; then the *cousins* chip in—and by and by everybody's killed off, and there ain't no more feud. But it's kind of slow, and takes a long time."

Obviously, that kind of feuding and revenge, Mark Twain's satire to one side, is adolescent and dangerous—and commonplace.

In today's scripture lesson Jesus was pleading, as he did in so many ways, for us to clear up the animosity or feuding that we feel toward our neighbor. Whenever a person wronged Jesus, Jesus looked upon the wrong as a sure sign of a deep need in the person's life. That is also Paul's meaning when he says, "Love takes no account of evil," *i.e.* does not keep a memorandum of injuries received, but tries to help. It was said of Christ that no one ever felt the full force of his kindness until he did Christ an injury.

When our anger gets out of hand we are in a condition best described as "The Mind Beside Itself."

The Christian view of human nature assumes that pep talks and cool reason are not sufficient to handle our anger. Cardinal Newman, preaching at Oxford in 1845, and differing from the optimistic views of human nature, was concerned to warn the congregation at St. Mary The Virgin that taste, intellect, and a gentlemanly upbringing were no match against the giants of passion—and those words from a man whose reasoning power was monumental!

Hate is one of the most consuming and frightening forms of behavior. I recall the dreadful story of a Dutch village that had been terribly tortured and wracked by the Gestapo during World War II. After the defeat of Hitler two citizens of the village debated what should be done with the commandant of the Gestapo. One man said, "My hate is so deep that I would tie him in a chair at one end of the street and run a line of gunpowder to the other end of town, light the powder and watch it burn toward the prisoner. Then, when it was but a foot away from blowing him up, I would stamp it out and cry, 'Let's do it over again.' " The pathology of hate, the hidden dynamics of fury, is such that some people love to hate, *love* to *hate*. Hate gives them a perverted satisfaction.

We like to retaliate in kind, especially if the offense is an abusive one. Let me illustrate by a story: a wild boar once invaded the garden of a farm. A hired hand saw the boar roaring down upon him, snorting and with tusks ready to toss him. The hired hand took up his four-pronged hoe and jabbed the boar until it bled to death. The farmer came back and asked why the hired hand had made such a bloody mess of the whole affair. "Why didn't you just hit the boar over the head with the blunt end of your hoe?" "Well," replied the hired hand, "I would have been glad to do that if the boar had come at me with his blunt end."

We do toss ourselves and others on the sharp prongs of our hostility. "Hate," said Harry Emerson Fosdick, "is as self-destructive as burning down a house to get rid of a rat."

At one time Congress was considering a bill to ban boxing, so many people were being hurt. Surprisingly, Margaret Mead, the anthropologist, testified on behalf of boxing, saying that we need such sports for spectators to ventilate their anger. That is, there is so much bottled-up anger in our society that we need vicarious ways of releasing it: boxing, hockey, football. It is a terrible fact that modern war serves, in part, as an expression of anger; fears and hates that we cannot contain we therefore take out on others. Nations have angry personalities just as individuals do.

I believe, then, that facing the truth about the reality of our anger and rage is the first Christian response: confessing that often we are more interested in saving face than in being reconciled, more protective of our pride than interested in restoring harmony.

The second response that the Christian should make to personal anger (and this is found in the scripture lesson for the day) is this: whenever possible, try to settle a personal animosity in person, face to face. Head into the center of the storm. Take the initiative. Whether offender or offended, don't let the situation boil and ferment. "Do not let the sun go down on your anger" (Eph. 4:26).

Our personal vendettas involve persons with whom we need to work through the hostility—not by running away, not by leaning entirely on an intermediary.

Husband and wife, parent and child, friend and friend suffer because of what has happened personally, and the gap must be closed in person.

Here is a story, melodramatic but true, of how two people closed the gap from both directions. It took place toward the end of World War II.

An English soldier sat down and wrote a letter to a German mother: "As a member of a party of Commandos raiding a village in France, it became my duty to kill your son. . . . I earnestly ask your forgiveness, for I am a Christian. . . . I hope I may, some day after the war is over, talk with you face to face."

This German mother received the note several months later, and in turn she wrote the English soldier: "I find it in my heart to forgive you, even you who killed my son; for I too am a Christian. . . . If we are living after the war is over, I hope you will come to Germany to visit me, that you may take the place in my home, if only for a time, of my son whom you killed."

The Christian effort to overcome anger does not always work: the desire for friendship may be rebuffed, the forgiveness ignored. It did not, or so it seemed at first sight, work for Christ. But Christ was consistent in his way of relating to people, praying and forgiving, and he did it with a strange eagerness and persistence. Thank God that, even surrounded by aggravations that seem incalculably difficult, we have the divine example of Jesus Christ.

6. On Pleading Guilty

The Parish Setting

Only a completely amoral person feels no guilt. I have never met such a human and, although it is claimed that such people do exist, it seems unbelievable that there is anyone (other than a mentally retarded person) who has no sense of right or wrong, and thus no sense of guilty failure. Since everyone in the church is a sinner, all feel guilty about something. This is true, I submit, even though we are adept at hiding many of our guilts behind a facade of self-righteousness or under a blanket of pretended self-confidence.

One of the most widespread types of guilt in every parish is that arising from a sense of worldly failure—to fail is to be guilty. This is a prevalent feeling even though, at surface glance, most of the people in the parish may appear to be successful. This particular form of guilt haunts ministers, no less. Paradoxically, the clergy are often the ones who are most judged (or who most judge themselves) by quantifiable, sub-Christian measurements of worldly success.

Perhaps the most pathetic example of such guilt is the once successful person who has had a brutal fall from the heights—the dismissed executive or the rejected parent.

This sermon, as I know from the comments of those who reacted to it, touches an exposed nerve. The sermon, however, only begins to get at an issue that bedevils us all.

The Sermon   *Text: John 9:24-41*

This sermon is about feeling guilty.

To begin with, I mention a weird bit of chemistry having to do with finding the age of Egyptian mummies. All mummies have blood stains. By the application of Benzedrine and Pyridine such stains will turn blue. The shades of blue are then analyzed by a spectroscopic device, and the exact age is determined.

I only wish that we had an equally accurate means of analyzing our guilts and thereby separating our guilts into the creative ones and the destructive ones. The good news from the pulpit today is that if we didn't have certain creative and stimulating guilts we would be subhuman. The bad news is that we have too many destructive guilts.

One of the caricatures of the church is that it is a place where people are compensated for their failures and guilt feelings. The church is seen as an ambulance picking up and rushing to God's hospital-in-the-sky those failures who can't "make it" in life. That may be a silly misrepresentation of the church, but it does raise from its roost a question that flies around this sanctuary and rests on the shoulders of each of us in turn, How do we as Christians deal with our personal failures and guilt feelings?

It will help us to deal with our personal failures and guilts if we disabuse ourselves of two widespread myths. It is a myth that there is or should be no such thing as guilt or failure. Each of us is guilty about something; each of us has failed. Furthermore, it is a myth that failure and guilt are necessarily the mark of a second-rate, an incompetent, or a bad person. Those myths are hard to dispose of because there is so much successism in our culture.

I am encouraged to see that at M.I.T., whose students expect to be successes, there now is a course in its catalogue on "Human Failure." I wish I had taken such a course. Like you, I have had incessant coaching from family, schools, and society on how to be a success. I could have used some advance preparation on how to deal with my failures. (Incidentally, I understand that the instructor in that M.I.T. course doesn't have the courage of his convictions: no fail grades are given, only pass and incomplete.)

Since failure and guilt walk hand in hand along with us throughout our lives, what are a few observations about the relationship between our gospel and failure and guilt?

The first and most positive and encouraging thing to

be said is to realize that both from a human and a Christian viewpoint, human dignity and civilization would not exist had we no sense of guilt and failure about the right things. Only those without a sense of right and wrong have no feelings of guilt and failure. The moment we have standards, goals, dreams, expectations, obligations we also, since we are not gods, have failures and guilts. (Only pathological monsters have no guilt or shame.) So it is that it is good news to have shame and guilt. "Yes, God, I failed, I lied. I gave in. I didn't do what is expected."

Only a morally blind world would be a world without guilt. "If you were blind," said Jesus, "you would not be guilty, but because you say 'We see,' your guilt remains" (John 9:41 NEB).

That is why we have, for example, an ancient prayer of the Christian church which begins with the startling words in Latin: *"O, Felix Culpa,"* "O, Happy Guilt"—the goodness of a guilt and shame that prompts us to moral improvement.

The other Christian reminder about guilt is this: to be mature human beings we need to rid ourselves of the wrong guilts and shames. How many people, how many of you here, have carried or are carrying loads of guilt and shame (exhausting, consuming psychic burdens) about matters for which you have no responsibility? To be guilty about the wrong things is as nerve wracking as driving a car with one foot on the accelerator and the other on the brake: i.e. trying to live well while crippled by the wrong, inhibiting guilts.

We don't have to be psychiatrists to know that each

of us, now and again, feels guilty over things that are not our fault, or that are irrelevant—actions of other people and other generations.

Some of these unnecessary guilts have a devilish hold on us; they are not easily shaken off. Many of them are formless psychic guilts, which lead to depression and self-hatred. They are not from God.

For example, I do not wish to carry around with me the weight of the mistakes of my parents and my ancestors. If my great-grandfather shot an Indian, it is not my fault. It is dreadful, as the biblical sentence says, "The fathers have eaten sour grapes, and the children's teeth are set on edge" (Ezek. 18:2). I do not want my children to feel guilty for things that I have done.

At its best, the church, by opening our eyes to Christ, is to help us distinguish what in life is worth feeling guilty about and which guilts are a total waste of time. Let's be very specific and personal. What are you after in life? Is it worth the chance of failure? Since none of us perfectly can achieve what we are after, there is some inevitable failure. I don't mind failing; but what would be too terrible would be to look back over one's life and to admit that my failures have all been in pursuit of the wrong goals. Or, to put it more poignantly, have our successes been cheap and shoddy ones? Have our successes, when judged by what we feel to be best, really been failures?

I leave it to you to answer this related question, Who has given Jesus and Jesus' gospel the most grief in life: the successful or the failures? In any event, we must never forget that Jesus was in his day a failure, judged by the prevailing success standards of 99 percent of his population.

To conclude, some guilts and failures are good, some bad. An experienced counselor coined this helpful epigram: "Guilt is the peg on which the meaning of being human hangs. It is also the peg on which the human too often hangs himself or herself."

A very large part of our ability to stay human . . . or to avoid hanging ourselves with useless guilts . . . depends on our staying close enough to Jesus Christ in order to see those goals in life that are worth success . . . and worth failure.

7. A Lively Time

The Parish Setting

There is a distressing form of pseudosuicide that is constantly appearing in pastoral work. I refer to the way in which life seeps out of living. Life, our most precious gift, is besieged by routine and gnawed at by boredom until life collapses into mere existence.

We cannot expect that life will always be pleasant, but we can always be "alive," that is, open to the wide range of joys and sorrows and the spectrum of human experience. To be alive means to participate, to care, to be aware, to make the effort, to drink it all in.

It is so disheartening, outrageously so, in the church of Jesus Christ, to see people let life dribble away. Conversely, it is enormously gratifying to see the church be that place where life is found and gladly seized.

This sermon originates in the juxtaposition of both experiences within the same church: Why does life shrivel up? and why, because of Jesus Christ, life expands.

The Sermon   *Text: Ecclesiastes 3:1-8*

There is no way to avoid the passage of time. According to Einstein's theory of general relativity, if you and I could travel away from the earth at the speed of light we would age only fifty-five years while the earth was aging three million. That's the only hope I can offer for any here who don't like calendars!

So, this is a sermon on how a Christian looks at the passage of time: God's metronome.

In ancient Corinth a statue of time has been unearthed, with this dialogue inscription on its pedestal:

Who are you?
I am Time who subdues all things.
Why do you stand on tip-toe?
Because I am always running.
Why is the back of your head bald?
Because no one whom I have overtaken, though he sorely
wishes it, may take hold of me from behind.

As it was in Corinth so it still is. Therefore, let us look at some attitudes toward time that are native to the Christian way of thinking.

First, it is a sign of human maturity and of Christian living for us to accept gracefully the passage of time. We are to be friends of time. That assertion sounds plausible enough, certainly; but think how often so many lives are a frenzied denial of time, fleeing it as if it were an enemy.

There are those who don't even like to have time mentioned. The ticking of the clock creates a deep anxiety, a reminder of mortality, and these people burn up valuable energy and money by fleeing time: with mindless activism, with cosmetic desperation, with sensate trivia, or with attempts to be young always.

Tennessee Williams caustically describes somewhere that for such people: "Fear and evasion are the two little beasts that chase each other's tails in the revolving wirecage of our nervous world. They distract us from feeling too much about things. Time rushes toward us with its hospital tray of infinitely varied narcotics."

Despite the general pessimism of Ecclesiastes, one does get the sense in those verses read this morning of the old gentleman in his club armchair, gently waving his cigar and saying: "My dear fellow, what's all this fuss about? I've seen it all before. Try and get some perspective on time."

I know that, as one gets older, it is not always easy to be reconciled to the passage of time. That is why I so admire those older people who, whatever their personal struggle, succeed in aging gracefully.

God entered into time. God created time. These days and years are not a prison. We not only can accept time; we should find in each of its phases a different kind of growth and satisfaction.

Second, another, and clearly distinguishing, Christian view of time is the determination to put time to good use. This does not mean, as some have sourly implied, that we are to have neither fun nor relaxation, or that we must always be grave and serious about each minute. But it does imply that, like our natural resources of land and air and water, time is not to be cavalierly wasted. It is at this point that we hear those New Testament readings: "Redeem the time," "now is the acceptable time," "making the most of time."

The chairman of a Student Counseling Service in Boston asks questions that cause students to perk up: Where do you want to be five years from now? What use are you going to make of your time? Another interview game often used in therapy sessions with younger people is this: write the following three dates across a page: your birthday, today's date, your actuarial life expectancy date. Now, make a list of certain specific things you wish to accomplish between now and then.

The Christian church and faith do urge us, without either melodrama or morbidity, to think about what we are hoping to do with our time.

Here are striking lines written as the Phi Beta Kappa Oration by Professor Theodore Spencer of Harvard's English Department. He was moved to the lines by looking at Alumni Reunion parades, seeing what had happened to former students of his. His poem "The Alumni" ends:

> If we could imagine all of time held to a single moment,
> Or even the last fifty years caught up in a momentary flash,
> And the round surface of the earth flattened to a square graveyard,
> Or even the space of this America shrunk to an acre in that graveyard,

> And in that moment, hovering above that acre, you and I
> Should listen to the expended human cry of all those people,
> The vast membership of the dead in all that time, that space,
> And all their local cries and complaints and regrets were
>   chorused to one
> Cry and lament and regret sighing through the echoing air,
> We would hear a single word only: "Unused, unused!
> Everyone seeing his life through time, through space, would
>   cry,
> Looking back in vain and in anguish, "O, unused!"
> (Theodore Spencer, *Poems: 1940-47* [Cambridge: Harvard
> University Press, 1948], p. 65).

While life flows with any vigor, while the mind retains any clarity, we Christians owe it to our Creator to give a good account of our time, remembering Him whose own brief life was filled to the bursting with hours of a lifetime richly poured out.

The concluding Christian conviction about time is in the reminder that you and I live under two clocks, the temporal and the eternal. The temporal clock tells me that it is now 10:15 A.M., Sunday, January 6, 1980. The other clock has no hands. We are also living under the aspect of eternity—eternity not as a vague, empty timelessness, but as a continuing, intelligent, changing growth from glory to glory, beyond our imagining.

In a graveyard in Burlington, Vermont, is this epitaph:

> She lived with her husband fifty years. . . .
> And died in the confident hope of a better life!

So be it! Our time on this earth is a time between the times, since we came from God and we return to God.

Such an understanding of the time-continuum heightens our appreciation of the present, while softening our anxieties about death. Which is to say that our present days are to be well spent and highly valued, but they are not to be fearfully clutched, as if this life were all there is to existence. If we don't keep that perspective, we are much more likely to be selfish, opportunistic, and more afraid of death.

This year of our Lord is but one year in a far more spacious calendar. We live from "time immemorial" to "the present day" to "years without end." Amen.

8. Aging and the Generations

The Parish Setting

> When I get older, losing my hair
> Many years from now,
> Will you still be sending me a Valentine,
> Birthday greetings, bottle of wine?

The Beatles touched an exposed nerve with the opening lines of that song. Each minister knows how much aging is on the minds of the parishioners. My guess is that if the libraries of the clergy were examined the most marked increase in any category of reading within the last five years would be related to the aging process and death.

The discussion groups and best sellers of today are replete with talk and with writing about life's stages. All age groups, including the young, are increasingly sensitive to life's chronology.

A church, which sees life as a pilgrimage *sub species*

aeternitatis, ought to be a very special place where the mix of generations provides an opportunity to be open about aging. A church can be that community where the amazing gift of life is jointly celebrated, where birth and death are understood and accepted as being merely the opposite ends of our growth continuum as we come from and go to God.

The sermon here is assuming, then, that aging is not a "Showdown at Generation Gap" but is, rather, an inescapable part of our mortality. Each age group has its particular problems and opportunities. All ages belong equally to God's providence. Anyone preaching in that vein will not suffer from lack of attention.

The Sermon   *Text: Matthew 1*

Earlier this century Fiji islanders committed suicide at the prime of life, believing that they would live forever in such tip-top condition.

This sermon asks us to look at the impact of aging on our bodies, minds, and souls. This subject is for all of us here, whatever our age. Aging is a lifelong process, and older people often forget that struggles and adjustments related to aging began the moment they were first self-conscious about the calendar.

The late Jack Benny referred to his age group (somewhere on the far side of thirty-nine!) as "The Ovaltine-a-go-gos." I estimate that every third television commercial is aimed at our aging anxieties. One evening in front of the TV I counted fourteen different aerosol-can-preparation advertisements: each designed to make me look younger—from toe sprays to hair sprays.

Aging is not a simple slope down which everyone slides at the same speed. Indeed, the notion of going downhill is often quite wrong. Aging should be an upward, maturing experience.

There certainly are Christian implications to aging. For example, it is an affront to human worth to make value judgments about other people according to their ages. Our society loves to know our ages and then to react to us, to deal with us accordingly. This is particularly true and particularly unfair with older people who are often looked upon as marginal citizens.

Here are some cautionary words from the book, *Nobody Ever Died of Old Age:*

> It seems that Grandmother, with her trembling hands, was guilty of occasionally breaking a dish. Her daughter angrily gave her a wooden bowl, and told her that she must eat out of it from now on. The young granddaughter, observing this, asked her mother why Grandmother must eat from a wooden bowl when the rest of the family was given china plates. "Because she is old!" answered her mother. The child thought for a moment and then told her mother, "You must save the wooden bowl when Grandma dies." Her mother asked why, and the child replied, "For when *you* are old" (Sharon R. Curtin [Boston: Little, Brown, 1972], p. 196).

One's dignity cannot be measured by years. In Psalm 31 we hear the lonely lament of an elderly Jew:

Be gracious to me, O Lord, for I am in distress;
My eye is wasted away from grief, my soul and my body also.
For my life is spent with sorrow,
And my years with sighing;
My strength has failed because of my iniquity,
And my body has wasted away.
Because of all my adversaries, I have become a reproach,
Especially to my neighbors,
And an object of dread to my acquaintances;
Those who see me in the street flee from me.
I am forgotten as a dead man, out of mind.

(verses 9-12a NAS)

All ages are equally valuable to God.

Another major Christian consideration about aging is that aging is a form of and an opportunity for stewardship—permitting us to maximize the unique possibilities of each stage on life's way.

A woman of forty remarked to an older friend, "I wish I could grow old gracefully, like you." "My dear," replied the friend, "you don't *grow* old. When you cease to grow, you *are* old."

Growth ceases, at whatever age, when we sit in our chairs rocking the years back and forth, clutching a coffee cup filled with cold memories.

Just as we are given the stewardship of time by God, we are given our various ages in which to grow. I have seen people of twenty or forty shrivel like mummies. I know those of eighty or ninety whose zest for life is a joy.

Compare our life-span to the face of a clock in which we live from 7 A.M. to 11 P.M. At fifteen years of age it is 10:25 in the morning. At twenty-five years it is 12:42

in the afternoon. In other words, by the time many finish their formal educational preparation they are already in the afternoon of life.

Growing *older* and growing *up,* alas, are not synonyms.

Let me close with a look at those biblical "begats," such as are found in Matthew 1: "Jobab begat Zilia, and Beriah begat Jakim," and so forth. True, we are a church, not a tribe. We are Mary and John and Bill and Tom and Eleanor. We are ages ten and forty and fifty and ninety. But as a church of Christ, we are all "begotten"; we are all tied together in the common lineage of faith that goes back to Father Abraham. We are all "begotten" of God and, in the name of God, we are to take care of and to honor one another, from birth to death, through ages of ages.

9. God and Pandemonium

The Parish Setting

I have never yet met a true monotheist—either in my parish or in the mirror. In addition to God, each of us Christians worships and serves other gods. This observation is a truism in the widely accepted sense that, if one's religion be defined as that which most deeply animates one's loyalties and energies, the supreme Holy, Creator God has within each of our hearts a host of competitors: money, power, status, self-serving, sex: whatever.

That such is the case is not a terrible indictment of our religious duplicity and hypocrisy. Most of us admit that the one true God is always competing for other ultimate loyalties.

This functional polytheism is a serious challenge to preaching. For most parishioners, as for most clergy, our "benign polytheism" is always ready to turn into a fanaticism or a monomania or a Judas. The sermon is to remind us of that sleeping or quasi-dormant group of demons within, who, if not controlled, truly create a *pan*demonium.

The Sermon   *Text: I Corinthians 1:4-25*

Religiously, we are double agents. Let me explain. I have not been reading too many spy novels.

If by religion we refer to what is most animating and gripping in our lives, as in the phrase, "her work is her religion" or "his God is his purse," it takes no arguing to demonstrate that we worship more than the one true God. Each of us follows at least one God too many: a secular figure or ism standing in the shadows just behind the chancel.

We are not consciously hypocritical about this, and you rightly would be very much upset if you were accused of having deserted Jesus Christ for a worldly deity. Nevertheless, almost without thinking, we have divided up God's Christ. It is the same situation that aroused the indignation of Paul: "It has been reported to me by Chloe's people that there is quarreling among you, my brethren. What I mean is that each one of you says, 'I belong to Paul,' or 'I belong to Apollos,' or 'I belong to Cephas' " (I Cor. 1:11-12).

God is still divided up, as is Christ. We follow the true God in Christ, plus another: a passion, a cause, a savior, a political loyalty, a pet conviction, a monomania.

Louise is an ardent anti-abortionist—a Right-to-

Lifer—she walks, talks, lobbies, dreams, invests all her extra money in this campaign. Anti-abortion is her secular Christ.

Frederick gets lividly red in the face whenever the government or unions interfere with free enterprise. He is a passionate believer in free enterprise capitalism. Nothing upsets him more than any infringement on it, and he will probably have a heart attack because of it. That is his secular Christ.

Arthur Salem is a organic food nut. He wants to live in a tree house and eat granola. Unless all of us, according to Arthur, stop eating white bread the world will go down the chute.

Henry Todd is a minister whose church is so absorbing, so important, so crucial to the salvation of the world that Henry will probably come apart at the seams if his church collapses.

So it is. Each of us lives within an ellipse. One focus is Jesus Christ and God; the other focus is the Republican Party, or antivivisection, or gun control, or civil liberties, or some other kingdom of our world . . . a second Christ. . . .

The story is told of a frightened citizen who lived in the days of President Monroe and was suspected of not being a true patriot. He protested to a mob that wanted to beat him up: "I didn't say I was against the Monroe Doctrine; I love the Monroe Doctrine, I would die for the Monroe Doctrine. I merely said I didn't know what it was."

The real Christ, the jealous God, wants us to be quite conscious of these other doctrines (Monroe or otherwise) that seize our lives. He wants us to keep them subordinate to the true God.

The only God, the jealous God, the God of Christ keeps these secondary faiths under critical control.

The military is another good exmple. I believe that a strong, up-to-date military striking force is necessary in this world, but as one who served for a short time in the military I also know how much of a god militarism can be, beyond criticism. Here is what I mean: "Dateline, Washington, D.C., Jan. 1977":

> The Navy is proposing to spend more than 700 million producing a new eight-inch gun that the General Accounting Office contends is so inaccurate at longer ranges that it uses up all its ammunition before hitting the target. The gun, designed for twenty-mile range, can't hit anything beyond ten miles. Yet the Admiral in Charge contends that it is a "fine gun," and that people should stay out of his Bureau's business.

That kind of uncritical self-infatuation with human programs and passions is found everywhere: in business, in church life, in families. The only force that breaks down that stupid pride is the very jealous God. If that God is forsaken, then our secondary gods reign, causing pandemonium.

Pandemonium is "all the demons," all the little gods. Milton's *Paradise Lost* describes pandemonium, the confused uproar of the fallen gods and angels. The demons are debating what to do now that they have been driven out of God's realm. One demon, named Moloch, suggests endless fury and enmity. Another, named Belial, is for staying mum. Don't let us attract God's judgment again, he warns. Let's just be ourselves. The demon Mammon goes one better. He says, in Milton's words, "What can Heaven show more?" We have lost heaven, so let's forget it and accept what we've got. This will do. Let us take this hell for our heaven. And that, as Milton sees it, is the final end of rebellion against God.

Our passions, loyalties, the drums we beat, the causes we believe in become demonic when we place them above Christ. When they are subordinate to Christ and Christ's God, under God's astringent judgment, then they are able to be ministering angels to the world rather than demons.

10. When the World Gets Out of Hand

The Parish Setting

Life brings us many wonderful surprises: a new friend, a welcome job, money in the nick of time, a gesture from a loved one, the grace of health recovered.

We are reassured, furthermore, by the comfortable routines and ordinary predictability of daily life. The bus comes, the office is there, the children return from school, the summer cottage waits, the next meal is on the table.

Then, the chill wind blows. The unexpected hurt occurs. Life is shaken by death, a crippling accident, a divorce, a child on drugs, a parent's alcoholism.

Under these circumstances the church, to be sure, is an ark of safety, but it is so on seas alternately calm and stormy. The sea and the weather cannot be managed. We are finally not in control. Our finiteness mocks, threatens us. It takes a steadfast trust in God to face the unmanageability of this world.

Every person in every church is now upright, now cowering, in an unpredictable world.

The Sermon   *Text: Acts 20:17-32*

Have you ever watched the TV show called "Candid Camera"? It is based on setting up ridiculous situations by which to watch the reactions of people who are unaware that they are being photographed.

My favorite program was a scene in a restaurant at a table with a flower in the vase. A man and wife sat down. And then, right in the middle of the meal, the flower reached up out of its vase, bent down, and started drinking the coffee. Day after day this scene was photographed and in each case the people looked around, embarrassed, to make sure that nobody else had seen them, and then moved away to another table and tried to look as if nothing had happened.

It was a foolishly delightful show. But it did emphasize that we really don't want anything to break into our tidy little worlds with the startlingly unexpected, the kind of thing we can't manage.

"The kind of thing we can't manage." That is a common experience which is ours, just as it was that of both Jesus and Paul. That is, we live with unmanageable futures. Paul said to the elders at Miletus, "Behold, I am going to Jerusalem, . . . not knowing what shall befall me there" (Acts 20:22). Jesus, facing his unmanageable future, said, "Father, if thou art willing, remove this cup from me; nevertheless not my will, but thine, be done" (Luke 22:42).

Many of our deepest anxieties in this world of churning flux are caused by the fact that there is no enduring tidiness and neatness to the future. We cannot manage completely what lies on the road ahead.

We think we are safely snuggled in the comfortable routine of life, pillowed with health or money or friends—our faith supported by the flying buttresses of family or church or another's hand. And then, with crackling suddenness, like a thunderstorm, those buttresses may fall, one or all: the family, the affectionate hand of the other, the money, the health. Not all at once, thank God, or irretrievably in every case, but with a harshness severe enough to remind us in Lent that we had better reassess in what or whom or where our faith is grounded.

This perverse unmanageability of life creates anxieties which we cannot fully hide from ourselves. Our faith will not spare us from distress or from being victimized by the future. But faith in God does reduce the weight of anxiety. Let me illustrate with three of life's unmanageable facts.

First, there is anxiety created in each of us by the unmanageable fact of death: the absurd, insulting certainty that each of us will disappear from the face of the earth. One of the most moving things about the enthronement of a Roman Catholic pope is a little ceremony in his procession to the high altar of St. Peter's. The pope to be enthroned is halted three times by the master of ceremonies to receive a small brazier of glowing coals upon which he throws a handful of flax. As it flares up and is gone in a puff of smoke, the master of ceremonies looks into the pontiff's eyes and intones the ancient warning, *"Pater sancte, sic transit gloria mundi,"* "Holy Father, thus passes the glory of the world."

I also love, for example, this true anecdote. The best crafted, most handsomely and thoughtfully written obituaries are in *The London Times.* One evening at his home the editor of the *Times* received a phone call from Lord X's butler who said, "Lord X sends his compliments to the editor of the *Times* and begs to remind him that Lord X does not expect to last through the night." I will bet my last shilling that Lord X was a Christian who had come to grips with the fact of death. He deserved his elegant obituary.

Second: there is the unmanageable fact of evil and violence. I am not referring to accidents. I mean the acts perpetrated by those who want to hurt someone else. Herman Melville, whose *Moby Dick* is America's profoundest commentary on this presence of evil, once wrote sarcastically about the incongruity of the cover of the parlor Bible in his home that was bound "in white leather, with peach embroidery and hummingbird's wings." Incongruous, because the massive testimony of the biblical story is its honest facing of evil and broken promises.

The reminders of this unmanageable evil are all around us. One uneasy sign, for example, largely unnoticed, is the fact that in New York City manhole covers are no longer used on many streets. Instead the openings are paved over, and crewmen jackhammer through to them when repairs are required. Why? The city is afraid of bombers in the sewers.

Our faith doesn't make evil any less terrifying. Evil causes our faith to tremble—not evil in the abstract—but personally felt evil, pain, loss. Yet the whole Lenten story is about love facing up to evil, not being surprised by it, not cursing God because of it, but using love to overcome it. Not only is my natural anxiety about evil reduced by my faith in God, but insofar as I am able to embody love and to display justice, the power of evil is going to be reduced in the world.

Finally, we can shed our anxiety deriving from the fact that the church is never going to be able to manage the world and the world's future.

One time a Sunday school class decided to play church with minister, ushers, offertory, choir, organist, and all. After awhile they tired of playing the game, as children will, and were wanting to change it. One boy said, "I know, let's play Jesus." Well, that was a new one for the group and sounded great. When the other children asked the boy to explain the game he said that one boy would play Jesus and then the rest would be mean to him, call him names, strike him, spit at him, tie him to a tree, and pretend to crucify him. That took a bit of the glow off the honor of playing Jesus, but the children went on with the game. After a few minutes of absorbing the cruelty of the other children, the boy playing the part of Jesus called a halt to it and in so doing uttered a profound statement. He said, "Let's not play Jesus anymore, let's go back to playing church."

I work and pray for the church, but our world is large

and tough and relentless in its self-centeredness. I am not going to waste anxiety because the church doesn't conquer. That realization permits me to put more into the church for the right reasons, because here our values are anchored, here the true God is worshiped, here we mutually sustain one another in an unmanageable world.

Death, evil, an unconverted world—those are unmanageable. It is the same experience we share with Paul and with Jesus Christ. It is the same, that is, if our faith is essentially the same. When Paul left Miletus for Jerusalem he was not downcast. He was a human being whose faith had counted the cost, whose vulnerability was accepted, and whose life was anchored in the risen Christ. Therefore, without self-pity and with a strange confidence he simply said good-by, "I am going to Jerusalem, . . . not knowing what shall befall me there." And he went forward with Christ into his own unmanageable future.

11. The Packaged Person

The Parish Setting

This sermon addresses an issue that is one of the most talked about in everyday life, from subway to dinner table to cocktail party. The hallways of life and the gatherings of aroused citizens are loud with genuine concern about the lowering of standards in life. Some voices, to be sure, are only the chronic complainers. But, for the most part, there is a sharp uneasiness at the widespread abuse of human potentiality.

The issues most cited in this indictment are the appalling drop in the performance standards of too many schools, the drug problem, commercial vulgarity, and the ominous increase in crime at all levels of society.

In any era the Christian church has a mandate to fight mediocrity and human debasement. We are to love God and God's creation with all of our abilities. We are to use our talents to countervail the leveling tendencies within the packaged society.

This sermon begins with a fable.

Once upon a time the animals had a school. The curriculum consisted of running, climbing, flying, and swimming, and all the animals took all the subjects.

The duck was good in swimming, better in fact than his teacher. He made passing grades in flying, but he was practically hopeless in running. Have you ever seen a duck run? Because he was poor in running, he was made to stay in school and drop his swimming class in order to practice running. He kept this up until he was only average in swimming. But average is acceptable, as everybody knows. So nobody worried about that, except the duck and his parents.

The eagle was considered a problem student and was disciplined severely. She beat everyone else to the top of the tree in the flying class, but she used her own way of getting there, not the teacher's way.

The rabbit started out at the top of the class in running. But he had a nervous breakdown and had to drop out of school on account of so much make-up work in swimming. Have you ever seen a rabbit swim?

The squirrel led the climbing class, but her climbing teacher made her start her lessons from the ground up instead of from the top of the tree down, and she developed charley horses from overexertion on the takeoff. She began to get D in climbing and C in running.

The prairie dogs apprenticed their offspring to a badger, because the school board refused to add digging to the curriculum.

At the end of the year an abnormal eel who could swim a little, run a little, climb a little, and fly a little was made valedictorian of the class.

Although the fable clearly was written to protest educational nitpicking, it has a pertinent meaning for this sermon. It is a reminder that Jesus Christ asks more of us than mediocrity. Christ gives us the Holy Spirit in order to permit us to rise above the commonplace. We are to use whatever talents we have to the utmost in the service of God. Christ made the same direct command in the parable of the talents, when he chastised the person who buries his or her abilities in the ground. Or again, we are not to put our lights under a basket. In today's scripture reading Paul picks up the same theme: "It is my prayer that your love may abound more and more, with knowledge and all discernment, so that you may approve what is excellent" (Phil. 1:9-10*a*). *Knowledge, discernment, excellent* are words that expect far more of us than slovenly discipleship. In short, this injunction to use our abilities at peak for the service of God and humanity is not off-the-cuff moralizing. The living God, who gave us life, wants that life to be stretched, expanded, fully utilized as best we can with what we have. The best use of our lives for God and the world is a Christian expectation, just as Christ gave fully of himself and his spirit, just as Christ poured himself out . . . so we!

But, you and I say, "I am not a genius. I am a rather ordinary, mediocre person." Not at all. For example, I am not able to play the violin. If I took lessons and practiced assiduously, I dare say that in time I would become a mediocre, passable, violin player. However, contrasted to the genius of Isaac Stern, I would always be a mediocre player. But Christ doesn't define mediocrity in that way for the religious life. Christ asks that each of us live, pray, serve at his or her best, that we play the violin or be a mother or a student or a doctor to the best of our ability. Our best in the eyes of God.

Elie Wiesel, the Jewish writer, tells a story about a faithful Jew, a just man, who came to a sinful town, determined to save its inhabitants from destruction. Night and day he walked the streets preaching against greed and theft, falsehood and indifference. At the outset the people listened and smiled condescendingly. Then they stopped listening; he no longer even amused them. The killers went on killing and the wise kept silent, as if there were no just man in their midst. One day a child, puzzled by the unfortunate preacher and feeling sorry for him, asked, "Poor stranger, you shout and you wear yourself out. Don't you see that it is hopeless?" "Yes, I see," answered the Just Man. "Then why do you go on?" "I'll tell you why. I am not sure to what extent, if any, *I* can change these people. But if I still shout today and if I still scream, it is to prevent them from changing *me.*"

Russell Lynes, writing in the August, 1966, *Harper's Magazine,* underlines the spread of mediocrity and conformism. His article, entitled "The Packaged Society," claims that more and more people in the world come packaged. The package, by and large, is designed to conceal its true contents or at least to make the contents look a great deal better than they are. Indeed, he remarks, "We are all items in a national supermarket—categorized, processed, labeled, priced, and readied for merchandising. . . . most of us like to wrap ourselves in a cover which will create a saleable package."

It is one of the central and amazing convictions of Christians that there is a God-given power, the Holy Spirit, which undergirds us in our efforts to give our best for God. When we live close to Christ we feel the interior animation of that divine spirit—the very spirit that was discerned in its fullness in Christ. Christ was determined to be obedient to God, not selling cheaply his one life, not flattening out beneath public opinion.

A parson in Scotland once presented a silly idea to his church deacons. After prolonged debate, the chairman of the diaconate gave in and said, "Well, Padre, your idea is absurd, foolish, and ridiculous, but you've persuaded me that it's the will of God!"

So it is with us when we offer only our second best. Can we swim, climb, run, fly, dig? Whatever we can do, we can do it well for the glory of God. For the sake of God let us not permit life to dehumanize us into dull mediocrities.

"It is my prayer that your love may abound more and more, with knowledge and all discernment, so that you may approve what is excellent."

12. On Coping with Grief

The Parish Setting

One day a fox chased a rabbit up and down the meadow but never could catch him. In exhaustion, the fox crawled back into his hole and complained of his hunger to an older and wiser fox, "Why can't I catch that rabbit?" "Well," said the older fox, "you are running for your supper; that rabbit is running for his life."

The emotion of grief, as encountered in both personal and parish life, may be defined as "people who are running for their lives." People suffering grief, a terrible hurt and loss resulting from a catastrophic event crucial to one's very soul, are behaving like those threatened by death. The pastor-preacher must interpret and listen and "be present" with all the tenderness and caring humanly possible. If the pastor does not understand grief, shoulder at least part of its weight, any sermon on grief will be a disaster.

Fortunately, there are many good books on the subject of grief. But, standing in the pulpit and addressing persons face to face is no time to be bookish about grief. The congregation must know and sense that the preacher has partaken of the grief, feels what is happening in the bones of the griefstricken.

So pervasive is grief in all lives (no matter how some may try to hide it) that it must be a constant theme of preaching. The gospel, God speaking through Christ, saves church, congregation, and pastor from the morbidity and heaviness of those whose grief has no consolation.

The Sermon   *Text: Isaiah 53:1-9*

Robert Frost, asked to define a poem, remarked, "A good poem, like a piece of ice, floats on its own bottom."

I wish all of life were like that, coming and going so effortlessly. But, however fortunate many of us may be from day to day, not one of us here will get through life without having to cope with grief. (The verb *to cope* derives from the old French, meaning *to withstand, to contend with.*)

None of us is wrapped in plastic, immune to hard blows. Each of us can sympathize with the parishioner who, with life's sudden wreckage all around, cried out, "I've just about run out of cope."

This is Passion Sunday: one of the two Sundays prior to Easter which memorializes the grief of Christ, "A

man of sorrows, and acquainted with grief" (Isa. 53:3*b*).
The next two weeks are to re-create the griefs of Jesus:
his agony—all that is contained in the words "for whom
Christ died"—his weeping over Jerusalem and grieving
for the certain loss of his own life. There is no way in
which we can take seriously Jesus Christ without
dealing with human grief, ours and others.

We are grieved in many ways: death, prolonged
absence of a loved one, physical disability, divorce, the
loss of a good life down the drain, the wear and tear of
aging, or the end of a career. In *Hour of Gold, Hour of
Lead,* Anne Morrow Lindbergh described her terrible
grief after the death of her kidnapped child, "Remorse
. . . is beating oneself in a vain attempt to make what
has happened '*un*-happen.' "

I am impressed, as I move about this parish and city,
by two reactions to grief: one, how magnificently some
people take the blows of life and, two, how hard and
unyielding some sorrows are.

Sometimes the blows of life have a staggering
unexpectedness, for example in 1923 at Chicago's
fashionable Edgewater Beach Hotel six men gathered
for a business luncheon. Among them they had
decision-making power over more money than there
was in the United States Treasury: (1) the president of
the world's largest steel company, (2) a member of the
cabinet of the President of the United States, (3) the
president of the Bank of International Settlements, (4)
the biggest speculator on Wall Street, (5) the president
of the New York Stock Exchange, and (6) the world's
greatest speculator in wheat and grain. By 1948 two of

those men had died broke, one had been released from Sing Sing, and three had committed suicide.

Passion Sunday, as Jesus moves from popularity to death, serves as a reminder of how suddenly the world can sway even for the innocent and the good.

There are several personal helps, strong aids, which our faith offers when we are forced to cope:

One, Christian realism that does not deny grief or personal catastrophe is a major source of strength. Jesus set his face toward Jerusalem—no whining, no excuse making. Our faith asks us to face death, to admit our mistakes, to recognize the problem. There are no shortcuts around Jerusalem; we must go through it.

Two, Christian maturity asks of us that we express grief. We are not to keep it all bottled up. Jesus wept. The more we try to contain our grief emotions, the more frustrating is any attempt to cope.

Dwight L. Moody, the famous evangelist of the late nineteenth century, once preached in Hartford. After his visit he wrote to a friend, "Hartford is a very poor place in which to cry." I hope we have learned better in the intervening years!

Three, in the Christian community we have a sustaining, sensitive fellowship of friends-in-Christ who do help us cope with our griefs and our sorrows.

The following letter was found in 1934 in a baking powder can wired to the handle of an old pump that offered the only hope of drinking water on a long and seldom used trail across Death Valley:

This pump is all right as of June 1932. I put a new washer in it and it ought to last five years. But the washer dries out, and the pump has got to be primed. Under the white rock I buried a bottle of water, out of the sun and cork up. There's enough water in it to prime the pump, but not if you drink some first. Pour it in and pump like crazy. You'll git water. P.S. Don't go drinking the water first. Signed: Desert Pete.

That anecdote is an example of how not to handle grief. Some of us, that is, never have primed the pump. We have gone through life gulping down immediate satisfactions but giving very little attention to the building up of a community of support, of faith, of prayer. Then comes the moment when in a great grief or distress we cry out for a cool drink of healing water and find that the pump has not been primed.

If this church truly has the Suffering Servant at its center, then the faith nurtured here, the friendships formed here, the prayer offered here, and the joys celebrated here truly become an oasis—a place in which to cope.

Finally, this last word from the New Testament. In one of his resurrection appearances there is this haunting verse: Jesus came and stood among them, and said, "Peace be with you" (John 20:26). And then showed them his hands and side.

He showed them his grief and expressed his solace. May such a peace be with you and with me, and with all those we love, in our good times and in our bad.

13. Mortgages on Paradise

The Parish Setting

I once heard Norman Thomas, the famous Socialist, assert, "Your faith does not consist in a long list of things which you do not believe." He uttered it wearily, after a long day's conference with ultraliberal skeptics.

This sermon responds gratefully to the warning of Norman Thomas because church life is always afloat in a "long list of things which parishioners don't believe."

The critical, skeptical approach to faith is a necessity for the inquiring mind. Yet Christianity is not a negative religion, and the preacher should not fill the pulpit with dangling negatives.

But, once in a while, carefully done, the congregation does appreciate, I find, a sermon which without judgmental finger-pointing, admits to fallacies and faults that have crept into the Christian tradition.

It is very important that the preacher put himself or herself *with* the people on such issues, not standing over against them. The minister, being as human as anyone else, must be very careful when dealing with the don'ts in the faith.

The Sermon   *Text: John 18:28-34*

"Taking the wind out of one's sails" is a nautical phrase that applies equally to that frail craft on which we sail: the ship of faith. We are sailing along trimly, pointing high into the wind, when suddenly our faith is overtaken by events that take the wind right out of the sails.

Today I hope to make clear, out of my own personal experience, a few major reasons for the loss of Christian sail power—those moments in my own life when faith and commitment are becalmed. I assume that what has happened to me probably has occurred to you.

So let me give you out of my own experience some examples of "wrong reasons for having faith in the Christian God." These are mortgages on paradise, if you will, which sooner or later are foreclosed.

One reason for a sudden weakening of faith—my faith at least—resulted from an overdependency on the faith of others. This is paradoxical, because a handful of remarkable people whom I have known helped create my faith in the first place. Was it not so with you? But there did come a moment of truth when I realized that I can't be a disciple of Jesus Christ by proxy; my faith won't grow beyond an adolescent stage, if it is in someone else's name. I must believe or not believe for myself.

Let me put the issue negatively. If the people whom

we admire do not believe in God, the natural tendency will be for us to be faithless also. There are as many atheists whose disbelief is as secondhand as there are secondhand believers. The opinions of the gang, the peer group, are very powerful. If our crowd is not particularly religious, we sorely will be tempted to drift in an irreligious direction.

I cite a psychological experiment that illustrates graphically the power of peer pressure in shaping opinion. A class in psychology had fifty students. Before the class met the teacher arranged for forty of the students to deceive the others. The teacher told them, "I am going to project two lines on the screen. One line is clearly longer than the other, but not by much. I want you to assert, in a class vote, that the longer line is equal in length to the other." Later when the question was asked in class, the forty hands went up, and then the other ten students, whose hands were down, slowly raised their hands.

How is our faith in that regard? Is our faith really our own?

Of course, it helps to have our faith supported and encouraged by others, but the convictions and the doubts must be our own. "Are you the King of the Jews?" (asked Pilate). Jesus answered, "Do you say this of your own accord, or did others say it to you about me?" (John 18:33-34).

Here is a second bad reason for Christian faith. To what extent is our faith dependent upon a sense of well-being, success, prosperity, good health—dependent, that is, upon making it in life?

A biographer of the Duke of Windsor, Alistair Cooke, remarks, "The Duke was at his best when the going was good." Is that true of our faith?

In Charles Dickens' novel, *Dombey and Son,* is this description of the manner in which the entire world revolved around the family prosperity:

> Dombey and Son, those three words conveyed the one idea of Mr. Dombey's life. The earth was made for Dombey and Son to trade in, and the sun and moon were made to give them light. Rivers and seas were formed to float their ships; rainbows gave them promise of fair weather; winds blew for or against their enterprise; stars and planets circled in their orbits to preserve inviolate a system of which they were the centre. . . . A.D. had no concern with *anno Domini,* but stood for *anno* Dombey—and Son.

Similarly, to what degree does our faith depend on good times and good health? It just may be that our theology is like that of Woody Allen the comedian, who accuses God of being "an underachiever." He writes, "I would believe, if only God would give me a clear sign—like making a large deposit in my name at a Swiss bank."

The third and last example of a wrong reason for faith, another mortgage on paradise, is also one which I have found down deep within myself. This is that faith which, almost unconsciously, keeps the wind in its sails so long as other people behave themselves. Oh, no, you may say, my faith is never so adolescent as that. But think again. Have you ever heard anyone say, "I would be a Christian and a church member if there weren't so many hypocrites in the church"? Or this from an American Indian of the past century, "White man no good; white man's God no good."

This bad reason for faith avers that God is made in our image. And that kind of god has no future whatsoever, because our image is never good enough for God.

A World War I grave in France has this marker: "In memory of Maggie, a mule, who in her lifetime kicked 1 colonel, 1 major, 3 lieutenants, 11 sergeants, 27 privates, and 1 bomb."

If we want to bomb our faith, the simplest thing to do is to have God's existence and meaning depend on a human being. God's nature and God's rule are quite separate from your behavior or mine. The lamentable behavior of Christ's own disciples did not cause him to give up on God.

These, then, I submit, are three cogent examples of bad reasons for believing in God. These are dead branches on the tree of faith, and they are for us to prune away:

1. A faith that is not our own, but another's.
2. A faith that flourishes in the bright noonday, but shuns the shadows of life.
3. A faith in God that flourishes only so long as people behave.

Prune away those dead branches; the tree of your faith will grow taller and greener.

14. A Religious World Record

The Parish Setting

Americans are born to think big, like the church in Dallas that serves Holy Communion buffet style.

The bigness attitude creates enormous barriers between us and Jesus Christ.

Jesus lived in a small, unimportant land. He moved within narrow geographical boundaries. He moved about tiny villages and, with few exceptions, spoke to and worked with mere handfuls of people. The modern corporation, the billion dollar budget, the extensive travel: none of the perquisites of contemporary American size and comfort were his.

The context of this sermon, then, is a point of view, a perspective that is ill at ease in the presence of a faith which originated in the individual souls of obscure people, which struggled against big principalities and power, and which had as its worst enemies precisely those people with inflated egos and dreams of grandeur.

It does bring one to a pause to contemplate how Jesus would have fared among skyscrapers and metropolitan anonymity and the Super Bowl mentality. Since most of us live in such a setting and amid a value system that thinks big, this sermon is relevant.

The Sermon   *Text: Matthew 18:24-33*

This book in my hand *(The Guinness Book of World Records)* is itself a world record. It is the "fastest selling book ever published anywhere in the world." For example, Veronica Snider of Stuttgart has eyesight twenty times better than you and I; she can identify a person at a distance of one mile. The smallest living object is a virus with a diameter of seven millionths of a millimeter. The largest structure in the world is the Ford Motor Company Parts plant in Dearborn, Michigan, which occupies seventy-one acres. And the longest sermon on record was one of sixty hours preached by the Dalai Lama of Tibet in 1969.

This sermon, which will be a bit less than sixty hours, is about how our values and attitudes toward people are in large part shaped by size. Since Jesus Christ possessed the rare ability to see people for what they truly were, regardless of how prominent or how lowly, I think it will be helpful to preach on this topic.

It is obvious, when we reflect for a moment, that our values are, indeed, shaped by the size of things. Most of us tend to be impressed by large size, often assuming that bigger is better, standing with more awe in front of

St. Paul's Cathedral in London than before a lovely chapel somewhere in the countryside. Others, in a revolt against the cult of bigness, are turning back to small groups, small economic units, even small families.

In order to perceive how size becomes a religious and ethical concern let's look at it more closely.

First, bigness as a value.

Each year I study with bewildered fascination those lists in *Fortune* magazine about the five hundred largest businesses. This year I also read about the one hundred largest insurance companies, one hundred largest banks, and one hundred largest retailers. Many of you here work for some of those companies. Some of you are laboring night and day as conscientiously as you know how to make them even larger.

I know of a very good regional sales manager who can't sleep at night because the boss has just raised his quota 10 percent for the coming year; and the sales manager knows that if he doesn't make the quota, he won't be promoted. Our society is suffused with values and strivings based on bigger and bigger accomplishments.

Albert Speer, Hitler's architect, records in his prison diary, *Spandau: The Secret Diaries,* a conversation with Hitler that relates to the power of bigness: "The church will come around. . . . all we have to do is to apply pressure to them. And our great Movement buildings in Berlin and Nuremberg will make the cathedrals look ridiculously small. Just imagine some little peasant coming into our great domed hall in Berlin. That will do more than take his breath away. From then on the man will know where he belongs."

Suppose you and I by some magic, not now apparent to me, could double or triple the size of our church membership and budget in the next two or three years—burst the church to the seams, enlarge the staff, burn the lights until midnight. Make no mistake, we would be in the religious press, and whether or not we deserved it, esteem for this church would roll in like high tide.

Let there be no doubt about where this shoe fits. If in two or three years this church should shrink to one-third or one-half its present size, I would have some real troubles with my self-esteem—whether or not it was essentially my fault.

Those are some of the common attitudes about *bigness.*

Let's turn now to *smallness.*

There is a best-selling book making the rounds with the title *Small Is Beautiful.* It argues the case for smaller economic systems, urging us not to be so obsessed with massive corporations, gross national product, and such. One reason the book appeals to a wide audience is because there are many who do feel overwhelmed by bigness and who avidly desire smaller, more manageable organizations and more modest goals.

A recent cartoon shows a Volkswagen dealer saying to a salesman, "Think big and you're fired!"

I think of a woman about thirty, not known to any of you, whom I shall call Hilda. Hilda rebelled against bigness in all its forms and all its values: the big spenders, the big cars, the big family. A few years ago Hilda's favorite word for all such values was "gross." To the dismay of her parents Hilda retreated in hostility from the world that had raised her to a commune of six or eight other couples who shared her values of smallness. They raised their own crops, wove their clothes, lived on welfare, and talked endlessly about the virtues of smallness and simplicity.

I have just been reading about a young minister in Vermont who got into all kinds of trouble because he thought his church ought to be kept small—restricted membership, if you will, open only to those who were fully committed and 100 percent Christian.

The conclusion I draw from all this, when I set Jesus Christ and his God over against these values and these gods of "size"—the Great God Size—is that I had better stop in my tracks for a moment to see how much I am being misled by false measurements when I try life on for size.

I take it, when reading the life of Christ, that size *per se* is not the issue, either large or small. I take it that self-esteem or human worth in the eyes of Christ has nothing at all to do with whether I am a rich young ruler or a despised tax collector.

Jesus measured people by their inner dimensions. He cared for everyone, of course: the wealthy, the powerful, as well as for the most socially insignificant. But he measures all of us, brings us to account, with a standard of absolute impartiality that has nothing whatsoever to do with our size. The obscure servant who buries his talents is judged as fairly as the religious leader who abuses power.

Do we give too much credence to a person or an

organization because it is big? Is a person with much power and money automatically a better person? Or, does liking life on the small scale make one better? Of course not. In either case size *per se* is not determinative. I know some extremely powerful and wealthy people who are, in my opinion, much better citizens than a little nobody who is filled with malice, and vice versa. Many unknown-so-called small persons do a much more glorious job in the Kingdom than some born to every advantage.

Like our Master, the Christian is called to be a carpenter, who is not so much concerned for the size of building as he or she is for insisting that the joists, be they large or small, be not warped but straight.

15. How Willing Is God?

The Parish Setting

Is it overreacting for the minister to take as seriously as this sermon does the common and sub-Christian phrase "God willing . . ."?

The assumption of the one using those words is that, if only God were willing, all would be well in the world. "God willing, I will make my fortune."

I think the sermon is justified. It is often in colloquial expressions that the real theology of the speaker is illuminated.

The words "God willing" thus assume the wrong answer to the problem of evil—an answer, as this sermon contends, not compatible with our Christian faith. God is *not* willing that so much misfortune abound.

The phrase "God willing" brings to the surface the question that never remains submerged, How can a good God permit evil and incompleteness?

No one sermon, no series of sermons, can ever answer that surgical question to anyone's complete satisfaction.

The Sermon   *Text: Job 37:14-34*

How often have you heard or have said yourself something like this:

"God willing, my sister will get out of the hospital alive."
"God willing, our family will hold together."
"God willing, I will be fifty years old next month."
"God willing, we finally will have our first baby."

Just how *willing* is God? That is, how much of what happens to us in life, or how much of what we do, is to be laid at God's door? How much does God will?

We believe that God is almighty, omnipotent, our creator, and the ultimate source of all being. Is, therefore, God also the secret agent in everything that happens, particularly the tragic and unhappy events (for it does seem that we are more inclined to blame God for the bad than to praise him for the good)?

By the same irrationality, I can vouch that many people are mad at the church (guilt by association) because they blame God for their personal misfortunes. I could cite name and case of people who stay away from church because of a grudge, bareknuckle fight with the God who, they assert, is responsible for disease, death, or Uncle Ben's loss of a job.

Here is a scene paraphrased from a contemporary novel. The pen is dipped in acid, and seldom has God been more morally assaulted: A father's young daughter is critically ill in the hospital. It is her birthday, and the father brings a cake to her room, only to find her in a coma. The doctor says death is near. As he struggles home, the father passes a church and, though he is not a particularly religious man, at first he has an impulse to enter and to pray. As he pauses outside the door he sees above the door the great Figure on the Cross, arms outstretched.

Suddenly the father takes the cake out of the box, draws his arm back, and throws the cake with all his might at the cross. (An episode in *The Blood of the Lamb* by Peter De Vries [Boston: Little, Brown, 1962].)

Reactions of that bitter type have been going on since Job shook his fist and cried out, "Surely, now God has worn me out."

I wonder if insurance companies still use the phrase "Act of God" when referring to a disaster of nature, with the assumption that since no one else can be blamed, we, for lack of a better alternative, might as well blame God?

There are three assumptions of our Christian faith that we need to remember when we say, "God willing."

The first is this: God is willing, has willed to give us humans a limited but crucial freedom in our thinking and doing. Therefore, we cannot blame God for what we do with that freedom.

It is a limited freedom, to be sure. We are enmeshed in a universe of physical law. We cannot jump off the

Empire State Building and will to stop at the twenty-third floor. We are also, to a great extent, creatures of our culture and society. We are Americans; we are male and female, children and parents, black and white. And all such conditions severely limit our freedom.

But, along with such limitations to our freedom, is the equally indisputable fact that we do have significant freedom as well—freedom of choice, freedom of values, freedom of friends, freedom of goals. We are free to take the road to the right or to the left, free to be Christian, free to worship or to curse God, free to sin. We are not marionettes tied to the fingers of a manipulative deity.

We have a limited but crucial freedom. We always ought to be grateful that God has granted us such freedom. The alternative, a robotlike determinism, is appalling and is beneath any concept of human dignity.

The second underlying assumption about personal freedom for Christians is this: God's own freedom is self-limited. God will not interfere to prevent our free choices from having their results.

One of the noblest medieval saints was Teresa of Avila, a nun. There is a delightful story relating how Teresa in her prayers one day complained about a bothersome Mother Superior, saying: "Lord, if I had my way that woman wouldn't be Mother Superior." God answered her wryly, "Teresa, if I had my way, she wouldn't be either."

The third and most important Christian assumption for us to keep in mind when we are tempted to indict God for the catastrophic results of our own misuse of our freedom is that God is at least as good as Jesus Christ. With that in mind, I rephrase the questions with which this sermon began:

Jesus willing, our family will hold together.
Jesus willing, I will be fifty years old next month.
Jesus willing, we finally will have our first baby.

Can any Christian conceive that Jesus would *not* be willing for such events to happen? So, too, we say of God. We cannot believe that our God, the God of the good Samaritan and the lost sheep and the cross could ever will anything that is harmful or malicious.

How willing is God? Whichever way we hold that question up to the light, we must contend with our significant freedom of choice, with God's not tampering with our freedom, and with the nature of the God revealed in Christ.

We have every warrant to believe that what God wills is always on the side of the lovely, the pure, and those things that are of good report.

16. On Living with Insoluble Problems

The Parish Setting

This sermon originally was preached in a convalescent home for the terminally ill. Preaching to men and women, most of whom are strapped in wheelchairs, is as trying a challenge as a minister can face. The requirements for an effective and Christian word in such a situation remind me of a class years ago at the School for Navy Chaplains. The instructor suddenly called me to the front of the class and said, "You are with a wounded man who has only two more minutes of consciousness. What are you going to do?"

I later amended the sermon to its present form and preached it to the regular Sunday congregation. It is not only the terminally ill who find that many burdens are unresolvable: fearful imaginings, passing hurts, chronic illness, a destructive marriage, grinding financial anxieties, a mental sickness are in our midst, in our parishes, forever.

I myself have had to suffer through nothing comparable to the agonies of some parishioners. That being the case, how can a preacher be more than one of Job's friends? Nevertheless, a word must be spoken, accompanied by the prayer that some true consolation of the Holy Spirit may speak through it.

The Sermon   *Text: Ephesians 6:10-20*

A team of psychologists, who study the national mood, claim that in New England the lowest morale is reached during the second week in February! Christmas is far gone, ice is underfoot, taxes are in the air, throats are sore. We are in the mood of the lady who was fatally bitten by a mad dog and was found to be writing a long list of names. "What are you doing?" asked her doctor. "I'm preparing a list of those I want to bite before I die."

This is February, and perhaps this sermon is not well timed. But I am sure that, since we all have tough problems, the subject matter of this sermon is real enough. It is a subject about which you and I want as much honesty and help as we can find.

There is a church in Scotland whose architecture vividly symbolizes the congregation's demand for realism. On the pillar just by the pulpit is carved, like a gargoyle, the face of the devil, horns and all, with his tongue sticking out at the padre. And those pews, filled with no-nonsense Presbyterians, are really saying, "We've come here with many burdens, and we dinna want to be fooled with."

I am speaking about the plain and simple hurting of people with ongoing serious problems: testy, hard, aching hurts that are there each morning, just as they were when we went to bed. These problems range from serious illness, to bereavement, to a cracked marriage, boredom, financial stress, parent-child strains, loneliness. One thing is certain about those who are here in this sanctuary today: at least two-thirds of us on any given Sunday have such a problem on our minds and in our prayers.

So, one of the many reasons we are here this morning is because we are hoping that the church, the Christian faith, can provide us with special help, hope, and endurance. That is a valid reason for coming to church. Paul, who had a long list of unresolved personal problems, including physical illness and public scorn, has these fine words about the sustenance he found in his faith and in his fellow Christians: "I know what it is to be brought low, and I know what it is to have plenty. I have been very thoroughly initiated into the human lot with all its ups and downs—fullness and hunger, plenty and want. I have strength for anything through him who gives me power. But it was kind of you to share the burdens of my troubles" (Phil. 4:12-14 NEB).

Paul, characteristically, *never broods over his problems as an obstacle to faith, but rather glories in his faith as a source of strength for his problems.* Paul was so passionately carried away by Christ that he literally rode over his problems.

Here you and I are in church with our unresolved problems. It would be revealing, and we might try this sometime: to take paper and pencil and write down the one, two, or six thorns in our flesh. What are the burrs under the saddle, where exactly is life rubbing against the grain? What is causing the sleeping pill, the anxious daydreaming, the short temper, the sullenness?

There are certain obvious things that need to be said about such a list. In saying them I don't for a moment want to give the impression that dealing with problems is easy or that I am, or that anybody can be, a neat solver of problems. But there is one matter to be raised with ourselves when we are particularly beset. Let me mention the one that scratches our ego. It is this, How many of us are willing to seek help from a friend, a psychiatrist, a physician, a minister, a husband or wife, or do we have such a stiff upper lip and such a sense of stern self-sufficiency that we won't ask for help? If that is the case, then add this to your list: one of my unresolved problems is that I am so all knowing that I won't be helped.

All right, then. What is the specific, unique contribution of our faith in helping us with continuing and burdensome problems? How do we weigh our faith and our problems in the same scale and do so as we keep an eye on the devil carved on the pillar, lest we become sentimental and soft?

When some people put their problems alongside their faith, trying to relate Jesus and God to what is hurting, they get quite angry, either blaming God for the problem or expecting Jesus to be a magician. Problems bring many people to the boundary line between Christian faith and magic. Christianity is not magic; it cannot solve or resolve all problems. God's providence waves no wand to dispel all our woes.

I have always liked these words from an English priest: "Christian faith does not free me from perplexity; it does enable me to live with a lot of unresolved problems." We have to say it straight out and stand at the foot of the cross when we say it: "I don't know why we have such biting problems, why God is crucified and people are hurt, but we do see Jesus, and we keep going."

It is true, of course, if we indulge in speculation, that Jesus and those of his day had to endure problems that we don't have to; he didn't have an outpatient clinic to which to refer the lame and the halt; the Gadarene demoniac could not be admitted to a mental hospital. The woman caught in adultery didn't have an encounter group therapy session. As for Jesus himself, what resources did he have? We know that he went aside again and again for prayer, and that his communion with God helped the most.

It is not speculation, however, to realize and to remember that Jesus had severe problems with which he had to live, and because of which he eventually had to die—the same sort that we have. He had the continuing problem of maintaining his character and integrity in the face of cheapness and dishonesty. He had the unending problem of facing bitter opposition without himself turning cynical. He had the daily problem of telling people that he was no military savior. He had the agonizing problem of betrayal among his own disciples. He had to trust in God and live with all those problems.

You and I are not Jesus. But God has not set small standards before us.

We must pray. Even when we are angry, even when we want magic to resolve our problems, even when we can't sort it all out. "It is your world, O God, and you are God, and I remember Jesus. Grant me, I pray, enough of your love and grace and strength to see it through." That passage from Ephesians which was read for our scripture lesson was voiced by Paul. He lived with his problems halfway, as it were, between the devil on that pillar and the face of Jesus on one opposite. And what Paul had to say is the most basic, the truest answer the *Christian* can give to the deep problems that beset us: "Finally then, find your strength in the Lord, in his mighty power. . . . Therefore, take up God's armour; then you will be able to stand your ground when things are at their worst. . . . Pray on every occasion in the power of the Spirit" (Eph. 6:10-18 NEB).

And we today are to keep the faith, to pray in the spirit, and to remember Jesus. When we do that a force greater than our own strength, like the tidal flow that lifts the stranded boat, rushes in and adds to our weakness its might.

17. On Cooling It

The Parish Setting

Preoccupation with one's own security, playing it cool, surfaces most dramatically in two areas: in marriages where, even after years of supposed intimacy, the two people have not learned to share and to let go of their feelings; and in the situation where we are so caught up with our daily work, keeping life on an even keel, that we fail to respond to human need.

The parable of the good Samaritan is saying, in part, that "good" people are so engrossed with their own well-being that they forget to care—that we "good" people are too cool.

Christianity is not a cool religion; but Christians, as I meet them and as I meet myself in daily living, spend excess energy in the attempt to keep our hands clean and our shirttails tucked in. One woman in my parish put it to me beautifully: "I was raised to dread a scene much more than a sin." When we are infected with that attitude we do, indeed, walk by on the opposite side of the street.

The Sermon   *Text: Luke 10:25-37*

Recently on a university campus the parable of the good Samaritan was repeated, with malice aforethought. A professor, impressed with how much distraction there is in the way of modern students' study, told his class that he wished to find out whether it made any difference in examination results if the students studied quietly and alone in a room or studied on the move in the midst of distraction. So he gave half the class an assignment to be studied in their rooms, in silence for an hour. The other half of the class was given the same textbook assignment and told to study it, also for an hour, while walking around the campus on a specified route.

The teacher was deliberately fooling his students. He really wanted to find out how compassionate they were. So he had "planted" on the walking route a student who was paid to act the part of one in great pain, rolling and groaning about. Well, the long and short of it was that only three out of twenty-eight students who walked the route so much as bothered to slow down or to evidence any concern for the "ailing" student, so intent were they on reading for their examination. Thus was demonstrated once more what had happened on the road to Jericho.

The students, incidentally, were all members of

the same New Testament class at the university's theological seminary.

Each of us has his or her particular reason or excuse for hurrying along on the other side of the road. These reasons seem to fall into major groups—two types of people who pass on the other side on the road to Jericho.

However, before describing those two groups, I would like to put in a good word for most of us, before God and this congregation. I don't know of anyone here who is always on the wrong side of the Jericho Road, impervious and unheeding.

I know that you help in many ways; that you try, and that you are sensitive to human need. If anyone absolutizes the parable of the Good Samaritan by saying that the priest, or the levite, or you and I are always on the wrong side of the road, with blinders on, is just plain being unfair. Jesus made no such accusation.

Our problem, rather, in the presence of Christ, is this, Why are we too often on the wrong side of the Jericho Road?

I submit that we can understand our answer to that question when we divide the great majority of those who pass by on the other side of the road in two very well-known human conditions.

The first group is the indifferent group—the sleepy, the apathetic, or what modern jargon calls "the cool." In Arthur Miller's *Death of a Salesman* the cool sons seem indifferent to the fate of their father. They are chastised by their mother: "He's not the finest character that ever lived. But he's a human being, and a terrible thing is happening to him. So attention must be paid. He's not to be allowed to fall into his grave like an old dog."

Indifference can stab the heart of the neglected. A child, for example, who senses that no one cares suffers the most terrible pains. How many lives have been seared because of the belief that no one cares?

This last summer I found a magazine ad describing ways of "keeping cool" in the summer. There is a certain analogy in these illustrations to cooling it in life:

> Keep a halved cucumber in the refrigerator to rub over your face and neck when they are hot and oily. This was a trick used by American pioneer women.

> Shower in warm water, slightly lower than the temperature outdoors. Then lather yourself with Truc's Suisse Savon a l'Huile de Noyau d'Abricot and imagine you're in a blossoming apricot grove.

> Keep quiet as much as possible. Turn off TV, radio, stereo. Get wall jacks installed so that you can unplug the phone. Stop talking.

> Sit in a rowboat in the middle of a lake with a thermos, sipping cider through a straw.

The simple analogy is that an uncomfortably large number of people do work almost as hard, if not quite as exotically, to cool it in life. Keeping cool, doing one's own thing, steering clear of involvement is a strong trend in our culture.

There are plenty of people in the Bible who tried to cool it: the Pharoah whose heart was hardened to the lament of the Jews; the Jews themselves later on who,

Ezekiel said, had hearts of stone rather than of flesh. Jesus' own life is one incident after another of running into people who, not knowing how to love or to care, or who being afraid to love or to care, retreated into cool indifference.

The second major group fast stepping it down the other side of the road to Jericho is the preoccupied, compulsively busy with agenda and routine. They are not indifferent; they are just the opposite: involved in life up to their ears.

The irony lies in the fact that most of those in this crowd are tied up with affairs of life that seem necessary: making a living, getting along, like the seminary students mentioned earlier.

Preoccupation can begin at an early age. A mother complained to several doctors of her five-year-old's failure to speak. Examinations yielded the fact that he was a remarkably healthy child, and she was told not to worry. But worry she did. One day, in a hurry, she burned his oatmeal but served it anyway. He tasted it, spat it out, and said, "God, this stuff is awful. You must have burned it." Delighted, she said, "You're talking! Why haven't you said anything before this?" He looked at her with some disdain and said, "Well, everything's been all right up to now!"

I have no easy answer as to how one balances all these absorbing, legitimate claims with the need to care.

But Jesus was undeviating: no one is excused no matter how important, or religious, no matter how motivated by the best intentions. The parable lashes the priest and the levite, persons of enormous goodwill and respect in their day, yet persons who had not found time to turn aside and to care. As a minister, I can visualize that priest hurrying along to the Tuesday luncheon meeting of the local clergy.

As I read the parable, I take it, too, that the person in need on the other side of the road may be someone right in our own homes, or in our marriages, or at work. That person need not be a stranger.

The insight of Christ is that we should never be so absorbed even in the good causes of life that we forget the well-being of others.

Anyone here rushing off to Jericho this coming week?

18. Christmas and the Real World

The Parish Setting

For all its glory, Christmas is beset, as one stands midst the holly and the ivy, by two deadly enemies. The most loudly lamented foe is, of course, commercialism: a Muzak "Silent Night" at Macy's. That enemy has been pummeled from every pulpit and decried from every pew for years.

The second enemy is more insidious because it emerges out of the very religious interpretation of Christmas. I refer to the heresy of "angelism," of disembodying Christ, of turning the festival of his birth into stained-glass poetry only.

Just because the music and the poetry of Christmas is so magnificent, just because the second chapter of Matthew is so enrapturing, Christmas tends to move off into the clouds.

A few years ago, in one of the many refugee resettlement camps in the United States, a social worker said to a small child seated atop a dismal pile of battered luggage, "Isn't it too bad that you don't have a home?" The child's reply was unerring, "Oh, sir, we have a home; we just don't have a house to put it in."

Angelistic views of Christmas provide no house, not even a manger. Both parish and preacher, then, are squeezed by two pincers at Advent and Christmas: the crass and the otherworldly. This sermon addresses this question, How do the sounds and sights of Christmas relate to the parishioner's "real world"?

The Sermon   *Text: Isaiah 52:7-10; Matthew 2:1-18*

Each of us fancies that we live in a very special place that we call "the real" world. This sermon will have a go at relating Christmas to our real worlds.

The challenge to the minister in a sermon such as this is that parishioners rightly ask that sermons be pertinent to their real worlds, that the sermon not resemble the ad for a new home for sale: "This home is very beautiful and twenty miles from nowhere." To preach to the many real worlds represented in these pews is a tall order. For example, a friend of mine told me that his son had a summer job, which consisted of cutting up hundreds of chickens each day on the assembly line of a frozen chicken company. What shall be preached to his real world? I don't know. About all I can do is to tell the fable about a rooster that was out walking on Christmas Day and came upon an abandoned ostrich egg. Never having seen such a large egg before, the rooster was flabbergasted. He rolled the huge egg back to the hen house with much effort, and crowed, "Girls, I want you to see what they're doing in *other* places!"

Real worlds: think about the variety of such.

A linebacker for the Detroit Lions professional football team writes, "My real world consists entirely of watching the feet of the opposing quarterback. I am paid $45,000 a year to watch those feet." A college senior throws down her history book and mutters, "I'll be glad to get out of here and into the real world." My barber's real world is fifty weeks per year of sideburns and scissors.

What do angels in the realms of glory, wise men, Herod, and a manger have to do with your real world?

Is Christmas, however delightful in its trappings and mood, only a fantasy escapist device? Here is a quotation from a man describing the impact of his uncle, who was an old-time, sawdust trail, stem-winder of a preacher:

> To listen to my uncle's preaching was like quietly getting drunk. He led his listeners into an unreal world of effortless peace, drugging them gradually into unconsciousness by the melody of his abstractions. We went home to eat Sunday dinners in a dazed silence and remained befuddled until Monday morning, when we woke up and went back into the real world.

Real means true, genuine, corresponding to what is—not imaginary. I put before you that Christmas affirms the most profound truths about life and death, about the nature of things, about what is true about human nature (both Herod's and Christ's), about what is worth living and dying for, about life after death, about what God intends. I submit that the Christmas story, like the rose window at Chartres, or a line drawing by Rembrandt, signals to us to stop and to consider if what we cozily call our real world is taking into account the larger dimensions. Christmas proclaims that, after you and I have made a list of all the things we do in our private and real worlds, we have only begun to touch the hem of reality.

A good education, travel, a variety of friends, wide reading—all of these enlarge our real worlds. Pablo Casals, at the age of ninety, would sit down each morning to play Bach and Brahms, and while he played he forgot his arthritis, his back straightened up, and he lived not only in the real world of Puerto Rico but in the universe. Emily Dickinson, dressed in white, living all her life in that home in Amherst, had a far, far larger real world than most of us ever dream of.

By analogy, and in the ultimate sense of "real," Christmas reminds us to expand our narrow definition of what is the real world. If Christmas achieves its intended result, we should leave this place saying, "Thank God, I have a cheering insight into more light and truth."

What do you make of these words from an archaeologist digging in the Near East?

We dug and dug until, at a depth of 60 feet, we discovered the remains of a civilization 6000 years old. It had begun somehow, flourished for a while, then had withered and died. It lay buried in its own dust. Immediately on top of that burial ground were the relics of another civilization, and so on. As I climbed up out of that pit sixty feet deep, with each one of my sixty steps I traversed one century of blood, sweat and tears. There—layer upon layer—was a cross section of human history, 6000 years of it. And when, at the end of the day, I reached the top, look as I might in every direction, I could see nothing but vast, empty, barren desert waste. And I said, "Vanity of vanities, all is vanity" (Henry Shorthowe, *John Inglesant,* vol. II).

Is that the final and real truth? Not by a manger-full!

This birthday party we call Christmas is, then, not an interruption of *real* life but the greatest and grandest revelation of reality. The reality of Christmas prevents our private worlds from remaining tiny islands.

The Christmas Bible stories are replete with people who were trapped in small worlds that they thought terribly real:

Christmas is God saying to Herod, "Your world of political climbing and cunning is viciously distorted. Its reality is cruel."

Christmas is God saying to the innkeeper, "Here is the One whom your busy world shuts out. Your reality is shortsighted."

Christmas is God saying to the wise men, "Here is a simplicity that needs to be added to the reality of your gifts."

Christmas says to all of us, "Wait a moment, please, you there, in all that feverish haste and that long agenda, just how much of God's real world are you living in? At your office, at your home, do your hear any celestial music; have you any time to see Him whom the carol calls 'Brightest and Best of the Sons of the Morning'?"

Christmas is the world's birthday party—the whole world—all of reality.

T. S. Eliot claimed, "We cannot bear much reality." We snuggle, therefore, within the familiar reality, limited though it may be. But Christmas calls us to a larger world.

When each of us leaves this church today for his or her "real" world, Christmas goes with us, gently but firmly tugging at our elbows and saying, "Thanks for coming to the party, thanks for the presents and the gaiety and the music. And by the way, when you wake up tomorrow and the week after, may your own world be more real and broader and deeper than it ever was before."

Listen, finally, to Shakespeare sing the reality of Bethlehem:

> Some say that ever 'gainst that season comes
> Wherein our Saviour's birth is celebrated,
> The bird of dawning singeth all night long;
> And then, they say, no spirit can walk abroad;
> The nights are wholesome; then no planets strike,
> No fairy takes, nor witch hath power to charm,
> So hallow'd and so gracious is the time.
>
> *Hamlet,* Act I, Scene I

19. On Going Aside

The Parish Setting

> When from our better selves we have too long
> Been parted by the hurrying world, and droop,
> Sick of its business, of its pleasures tired,
> How gracious, how benign, is Solitude.

Wordsworth's determination to seek "benign" solitude is not matched, however, by the average parishioner (or minister?) who plunges into time-off with the intensity of an Olympic high-diver.

A man hitchhiking to the Mardi Gras was picked up by a driver who noticed that his passenger was carrying a Bible. The driver asked, "Where are you going?" "To the Mardi Gras. I understand that is a wide-open town. I'm going to spend all my money, go to night clubs, drink too much, gamble and paint the town red." "Well, good luck," the driver replied. "By the way, what's the Bible for?" "Oh," the hitchhiker said, "if things go well, I might stay over until Sunday."

So it is. It may well be that the typical vacation is neither refreshing nor different in basic tempo from the regular day's schedule. In any event, a myth of parish life, as of American life generally, is that vacationing is spiritually nourishing. The evidence for that is slim.

To be alone with God, in church or out of church, is virtually nonexistent in parish life. Church life and programming may itself, indeed, be as cannibalizing of solitude as the surrounding culture. Which is why Karl Barth said, "Our last hiding place from God may be the church."

A sermon dealing with the frantic activity of our vacations will most certainly speak to a profound human need, but the sermon must be reinforced with small group retreats and other disciplines that strengthen even the best of intentions.

The Sermon   *Text: Genesis 1–2:3*

The occasion for this sermon is my realizing that you parishioners take as many winter vacations as summer vacations. We seek, whenever we can find it, a rhythm between work and rest. There is a parallel and, even more necessary, alternation between busyness and spiritual refreshment. Spiritual refreshment is, however, not by any manner of means to be equated with vacation or respite from daily work.

This whole issue brings to mind a farmer out near

Skowhegan, Maine, near where I once lived. He said, "There are three things I don't like: digging potatoes, chopping wood, and work." This amply proves that great minds may differ as to what constitutes rest and what is work!

In any event, we need not confuse vacations or timeoff with the religious practice of inwardness, worship, and tranquil solitude in the presence of God.

In Princeton, New Jersey, I knew a taxi driver who worked long hours behind the wheel for fifty weeks a year. Then, with his profit, he and his wife would go to Las Vegas. He would give her half the money, keep the other half, and then each would play the slot machines for sixteen hours per day, return home, and he would get behind the wheel again. Or, many here may have had the experience of driving a station wagon full of children to the Grand Canyon, only to have them sit on the rim of all that splendor and read Batman comics.

Whatever we do in the name of fun and games, there remains a basic unfinished need of the soul that in most instances is not satisfied by mere change of pace or vacation.

In the Gospel stories Christ constantly withdrew from the world, just as in Genesis even God is portrayed as resting. Christ was always "going apart," "going aside" by himself and, on stated occasions, joining in the synagogue Sabbath.

The Christian attitude to work and activity should be, then, what the Quakers call "centering down" or what Wordsworth termed "the Harvest of the Quiet Eye."

Spiritual renewal is a discipline that is hard to come by in our world. As an example, I recently saw an advertisement showing a suburban home, the owner of which has purchased a stereo system that plays different music simultaneously in every room: Rock music by the swimming pool, the Boston Pops in the patio, Bach in the den, Frank Sinatra in the bedroom, Gershwin in the greenhouse. The ad is symbolic of a Muzak culture in which no one can bear to be alone.

The saddest news item, surely, is this one from the *New York Times:* "Canned music has been installed in the Sistine Chapel." Apparently even Michelangelo needs accompaniment.

Saul Bellow, the writer, in a Commencement address, had this to say about the din of our culture:

> The one force which opposes the best in America is "The Great Noise." By noise I mean not simply the noise of technology, the noise of money or advertising and promotion, the noise of the media, but the terrible excitement and distraction generated by the crises of modern life . . . in short the sounds of the public sphere, the din of politics, the turbulence and agitation that set in about 1914 and have now reached an intolerable volume.

The outer noises of business, social, family, and political turbulence are matched by the inner noises of anxiety, fear, and frustration. This combined tempo will devastate those who never learn "to go aside." They are like King Edward VII who could not stand inactivity. During the last twenty years of his life he dined alone with his wife only once.

As you read the Gospels we will find, over and again, a line such as this: "Perceiving then that they were about to come and take him by force to make him king, Jesus withdrew again to the mountain by himself" (John 6:15). Or, as in Genesis, God Almighty, the Creator of heaven and earth rested.

As the years go by we are all ensnared by duties and jobs and routines. The agenda weaves its web around us. So, it is good to read this verse: "Jesus withdrew *again* to the mountain by himself." (Italics mine.) In that regard, most of us are found wanting. We may, I hope, enjoy moments of lassitude or of gazing at a sunset. Those times have their place, as with Petrarch when he came to Vaucluse in Provence to stare silently into that beautiful grotto:

> Here I silently sit and dream.
> No sound comes in, except when the stream
> Glassily whispers on its bed of sand,
> Or wind makes the papers shift in my hand.

That is fine, whether in France or Vermont or by the fireside. But when Jesus went aside he was consciously reviewing, thinking, praying about what he was doing the rest of the time—sorting things out, centering down, being with his Creator.

Bruce Catton, in his Civil War book, *This Hallowed Ground,* says of Lee's army approaching Gettysburg: ". . . scooping up supplies from the fat Pennsylvania farming country . . . lacking a supply line, it must eternally keep moving, because if it did not it would starve." That is an almost perfect picture of how great hordes of restless people live their lives: lacking any supply lines to God, they keep eternally moving on their own, compelled by the expediency of every passing hour, living entirely off of whatever resources they find in the ticktock of each moment.

I hope, then, that in addition to the bliss of necessary laziness or time-off, that all of us will find time for solitary reflection and prayer—each in his or her own way, and with God as our only company.

Our souls need a home, occasions which knit together our loose ends, to give a pattern to living. "Everybody must build a home for his or her soul . . . it is the source of security for integrity of conscience, for whatever inkling we attain of eternity" (attributed to Rabbi Abraham Herschel).

> Dear Lord and Father of mankind,
> Forgive our foolish ways;
>
> Take from our souls the strain and stress,
> And let our ordered lives confess
> The beauty of thy peace.
>   John Greenleaf Whittier

20. Living with Fear

The Parish Setting

During the early days of the Berlin Wall an incident occurred that painfully exemplifies the power of fear. A group of East Germans was tunneling under the wall when suddenly the leader became catatonic with fear of capture. Fortunately, there was a physician present who was able to inject a syringe of muscle relaxant into the leader so that he was able to proceed.

Although that incident is melodramatic, it does not exaggerate the demonic power that fear of one sort or another exercises in every life. I speak only of the unhealthy fears, not of those which we need in order to survive, such as fear of fire.

Fear is no less powerful for being subtle or for being disguised behind bravado. I have met only a handful of persons for whom some fear was not a critical issue—the fear of loss of money, of face, of status.

In counseling, as in daily friendship, such fears may

be great engines that motivate or drive one to accomplishment. But, in the long haul, the fears are self-destructive if not put in the perspective of faith.

These fears, dig wherever the minister will in himself or others, abound everywhere in the parish soil.

The Sermon   Text: Matthew 6:22-34; I John 4:13-21

The most famous magician in American history was Harry Houdini. He was the greatest escape artist of all time. His favorite breathtaker and heart-stopper was to have eight police chiefs lock him inside a trunk, with his arms and legs enmeshed in chains and padlocks. Then Houdini would be dumped into the East River, and he would emerge miraculously.

I mention Houdini and his chains because many people are in fetters to their fears, as tightly as if they were locked inside a trunk but, unlike Houdini, they don't know how to escape, even how to get one arm or leg free—and thus they drown.

Today I want to preach about the relationship between fear and the Christian life. For one of the most demonstrable results of trusting in the God of Jesus Christ is that we are freed from fear. I do not say that we don't have fears, or that fears do not plague us; they do. But Christian living is carried on outside the domination, the clutches, of fears.

The Greek word for fear is *phobia*. It is startling to learn of the wide variety of phobias which cripple. Here in Connecticut there is a "Phobia Center" where such disabling anxieties are treated. The most common fears are fear of death, fear of aging, fear of ill-health, fear of loss of money, fear of loss of status, and fear of not being loved or being popular. In addition to those fears there are these exotic phobias:

Optophobia:	fear of opening one's eyes
Monophobia:	fear of being alone
Xenophobia:	fear of strangers
Decidiophobia:	fear of deciding

or this rare and delicious phobia: *Arachibutrophobia:* fear of peanut butter sticking in one's mouth.

I have a friend in Boston, a lovely lady, whose eccentricity is a phobia about germs. She doesn't like to shake hands, and the moment her guests leave her parlor she goes into a frenzy of brushing and vacuuming the chairs and couches.

Dudley Cavert tells a true story of a railway employee in Russia who accidentally locked himself in a refrigerator car. He was unable to escape and couldn't attract the attention of those outside, and so he resigned himself to his fate. As he felt his body becoming numb, he recorded the story of his approaching death in sentences scribbled on the wall of the car. "I'm becoming colder," he wrote. "Still colder, now, nothing to do but to wait. . . . I am slowly freezing to death. . . . Half asleep now, I can hardly write . . ." And finally, "These may be my last words."

And they were, for when at length the car was opened they found him dead. And yet the temperature of the car was only fifty-six degrees. The freezing apparatus was out of order. There was no physical reason for his death. There was plenty of air; he hadn't suffocated. He was the victim of his own phobia.

"Perfect love casts out fear" (I John 4:18*b*). Jesus said, "Sufficient unto the day is the evil [or the problem] thereof" (Matt. 6:34*b* KJV). Clearly, those who trust in God, who are seeing the world through the eyes of Christ, are not *enslaved* to fears. We are, of course, often afraid and even ridden by trepidations, but Christian living is not essentially fearful living. It is trusting, open, adventuresome living. The fearful person is so demanding of security and peace and well-being, so prudent, that he or she lives within a cocoon, spun by the iron web of one fear after another. Jesus said, "Whoever would save his life will lose it" (Matt. 16:25). Jesus did not say, as so many well-meaning people do, "Don't worry." He said, "Let not your hearts be troubled; believe in God, believe also in me" (John 14:1).

Jesus was, in effect, saying, "You can't handle it all; if you try, you will collapse. You will be so inhibited with self-safety that you won't live, can't live. God lives. Let God handle life. Do your best, but don't try to carry the universe on your shoulders."

"Sufficient unto the day is the evil thereof." Don't stay in a fetal position all your life. Don't be so protective, with your arms hugging yourself. Have some abandon and trust.

A Dominican friar said to a group of young priests, "If you don't stop being so careful, you will die in your beds, and it will serve you right."

Wouldn't it be wonderful if we could have two offertories each Sunday: one for the money and the other into which we could empty our worries and fears? We are so burdened with fear, illusory or real.

In Africa there is a lake where the fishermen have a unique way of catching the fish. At noon the fishermen go out with a long line tied between the boats. To this line, at short intervals, are attached wooden floats. The sun, shining overhead on the clear waters, sends shadows of these floats right to the bottom, and the fish eye view, apparently, is that of a series of bars running from the surface to the bottom. Gradually, the fishermen tow the floats to shore, with the fish being driven before these insubstantial bars, until the fish come to the shallow water where the men stand and throw the fish ashore.

Well, fellow fish, how many of our fears and anxieties are illusory, luring us to be captured?

Jesus, we know, felt fear, but he had so much love and trust that he lived and died unfettered by fear—fear had been cast out by obedience. The major fear of Jesus, I suggest, was that he would not have enough strength and courage and love to be the suffering servant Messiah, for to be that meant unhorsing all kinds of possessive demons. The one, for example, that whispers in our ears, as it did in Jesus', "Do you not want to be a popular hero to all these people around you? . . . Jesus, do you not want to be a political Messiah and lead a violent revolt against Rome?"

I am sure that those disciples who turned aside from the fearful securities of a tightly controlled life to follow

Christ saw a different vision, felt a new love, responded to a glorious new music. The old fears tumbled off their backs and, as they felt the new freedom in Christ, they must have asked themselves, "Why did I carry the burden of those fears for so long?"

For surely, when we clutch a style of life which is designed and dictated by our fears, rather than by our loves, we find ourselves immersed in a monotonous, dreary, second-rate scenario.

Is that the way we want it to be? It can be so much better, more adventuresome, satisfying, fulfilling, and fearless. "Perfect love casts out fear."

On the mantel of an old English wayside inn is carved this motto: "Fear knocked at the door, faith answered, no one was there."